The Art of Selective Attention

Master Your Concentration,

Set Boundaries,

Overcome Distractions, and

Transform Your Life With

Mindful Focus.

ARUN KUMARA KHANDA

https://arunkumarrk.com

YOUR FREE GIFT

As a token of my gratitude for taking out time to read my book, I would like to offer you a free gift.

Click the below link or scan the QR code to download your free eBook PDF

https://arun-kumar-khanda.ck.page/00c46de54c

Gratitude

In my author journey, many blessings count toward my success. I am thankful to my mentor and bestselling author **Mr. Som Bathla** for mentoring, motivating, and guiding me to write, self-publish, and launch books on my way to the autho-preneur journey. I am also thankful to my author community, especially Sooraj Achar, the bestselling author, for his timely technical support, encouragement, and advice to make my work easy. I am grateful to my readers for their support. I am happy to offer my gratitude to Amazon Platform for the huge facilities given to the authors for transforming the lives of millions. The readers can connect with the author at akhanda1969@gmail.com

CONTENTS

Preface

In a world flooded with information, distractions, and endless demands on our time, the ability to focus our attention on what truly matters has become an invaluable skill. This book, **"The Art of Selective Attention,"** explores the profound art of intentionally choosing where we direct our mental energy, offering insights and practical strategies to help you regain control over your attention and transform your life.

Chapter by chapter, we embark on a journey into the intricate realm of selective attention, understanding its science and the pivotal role it plays in our daily lives. Through this exploration, you'll gain a deeper insight into how the mind filters through the myriad of stimuli, and how you can harness this power to your advantage.

In *Chapter 1,* we delve into the core principles of selective attention, examining how we make choices about what to attend to and what to ignore. Cognitive load, an often underestimated factor, is also explored as we begin to unravel the intricacies of our focus.

Chapter 2 takes us on a quest to understand distractions in all their forms and the nature of their influence. You'll learn practical strategies to manage and ultimately benefit from ignoring distractions, enabling you to find your focus in a world filled with interruptions.

Chapter 3 tackles the challenge of information overload and provides you with techniques to filter out the noise, focusing on what truly matters. It is within these pages that you'll discover the art of prioritizing information and gaining control over the deluge of data that surrounds us.

In *Chapter 4*, the power of mindfulness becomes your ally in the battle against distractions. You'll learn how to incorporate mindfulness into your daily routine, offering you the clarity and mental fortitude needed to navigate an increasingly chaotic world.

Chapter 5 helps you strike a balance between attention and obligation, guiding you to set boundaries and prioritize your precious time and energy effectively. The fine line between ignoring and neglecting becomes clearer as you develop strategies to find harmony in your responsibilities.

Chapter 6 illuminates the significant impact of your mindset on your ability to ignore distractions. By mastering the techniques to combat negative thoughts and self-talk, you will empower yourself to embrace the power of positive thinking.

In *Chapter 7*, you'll discover the liberating art of saying no, which enables you to confidently set boundaries, overcome guilt, and prioritize your well-being. The benefits of reclaiming your time and energy are profound and far-reaching.

Chapter 8 beckons you to embrace your own path and purpose, even in the face of the formation of external opinions and pressures. Strategies to align with your true self and find your passion are shared, providing you with the guidance to navigate your unique journey.

Chapter 9 delves into the essential need to create space for creativity and connection. You'll explore the impact of technology on these aspects of life and learn the advantages of disconnecting from the digital world to nurture your creative spirit.

Chapter 10 addresses the challenge of staying informed about current events without becoming overwhelmed. Discover effective strategies for maintaining perspective and finding balance in an era of constant news and information.

Finally, in *Chapter 11*, we conclude our journey by examining the art of ignoring for inner peace and contentment. Techniques to cultivate a mindset of letting go and embracing the present moment are shared, offering you the keys to finding true tranquility.

"The Art of Selective Attention" is a comprehensive guide for anyone seeking to reclaim their focus, reclaim their time, and rediscover the power of deliberate attention. It's a roadmap to help you navigate the complexities of modern life with grace and intention, enabling you to create a life where your attention is your most valuable asset. We invite you to embark on this transformative journey, embrace the art of selective attention, and experience a richer, more fulfilling life.

Chapter: 1

The Science of Attention and Focus

"But if we want to find what is hidden, we must seek it with the side of life that is turned away from us." - Rainer Maria Rilke

The Science of Attention and Focus:

In the age of science and technology, everyone is eager to see the science angel in every aspect of our lives. Whether it is love life or spiritual aspect, everywhere science is putting its nose. Science always takes the front seat in any discussion when the matter is the subject of discussion. However, now in the matter of relationships, cultural functioning, cultivating mindset, and even spiritual awakening science has made its entry. Now come to the topic. The science of attention and focus is a complex and fascinating field of study. Researchers in this field seek to understand the cognitive processes that allow humans to selectively attend to certain stimuli and ignore others. These tendencies may cost humans to some extent. This inference may not be applicable to all.

Attentional Control: How We Control Our Attention and Focus, and What Factors Influence Our Ability to do so:

Attentional control refers to the cognitive ability to regulate one's attentional focus and select which stimuli to attend to and which to ignore. It is the process of directing and sustaining attention to a particular task or stimuli while inhibiting distractions or irrelevant information.

Attentional control is essential for various cognitive processes, including working memory, problem-solving, decision-making, and learning. It is also crucial for everyday activities such as driving, walking, reading, playing, eating, loving, attending official duty for earning, and social interactions.

The research says about some areas of brain regions associated **with attentional control.** They include the prefrontal cortex, anterior cingulate cortex, and parietal cortex. **The prefrontal cortex** is responsible for planning and executing goal-directed behavior, while the **anterior cingulate cortex** is involved in detecting and resolving conflicts in attentional focus. **The parietal cortex** plays a critical role in spatial attention and orienting.

Spatial attention is the ability to focus our attention on a specific location in space. This allows us to selectively process visual information and ignore irrelevant stimuli. Spatial attention is essential for many everyday activities, such as driving, reading, and playing sports.

Orienting is the process of shifting our attention to a new location in space. This can be done either voluntarily (endogenously) or involuntarily (exogenously).

- Endogenous orienting is controlled by our own goals and intentions. For example, if we are looking for a friend in a crowd, we can voluntarily orient our attention to the area of the crowd where we expect to find them.

- Exogenous orienting is triggered by external stimuli, such as a sudden flash of light or a loud sound. When we hear a loud sound, we will automatically orient our attention to the location where the sound came from.

Spatial attention and orienting are closely related. Orienting is often the first step in spatial attention. Once we have oriented our attention to a location, we can then focus our attention on that location and process the visual information there.

For better appreciation let us see some examples of spatial attention and orienting:

- When you are driving, you need to orient your attention to the road ahead of you. Once your attention is oriented to the road, you can focus your attention on specific objects, such as other cars, pedestrians, and traffic signs.

- When you are reading, you need to orient your attention to the next line of text. Once your attention is oriented to the next line, you can focus your attention on the individual words and letters.

- When you are playing soccer, you need to orient your attention to the ball and the other players on the field. Once your attention is oriented to the ball, you can focus your attention on hitting it or catching it.

Spatial attention and orienting are complex processes that involve many different brain areas. Researchers are still learning about how these processes work and how they are impaired in neurological disorders.

Spatial attention and orienting are essential for many everyday activities. By understanding how these processes work, we can better appreciate our own ability to see and interact with the world around us.

Deficits in attentional control can give rise to many serious personal and social issues. Attentional disorders such as ADHD, (Attention-Deficit/Hyperactivity Disorder) are neurodevelopmental conditions that affect a person's ability to regulate their attention, impulses, and sometimes their activity level. These disorders typically manifest in childhood and can persist into adulthood. ADHD is one of the most well-known and studied attentional disorders.

People with ADHD often have difficulty sustaining attention on tasks or activities. They may be easily distracted by irrelevant stimuli and have trouble organizing and completing tasks. This can lead to careless mistakes, forgetfulness, and difficulty following instructions. Some individuals with ADHD exhibit hyperactive behavior. They may have trouble sitting still, frequently fidget, talk excessively, or engage in physical restlessness. This hyperactivity can be disruptive in various settings, such as school or work.

Impulsivity refers to acting on impulse without thinking through the consequences. People with ADHD may come out with an answer before a question is complete, interrupt others, or have difficulty waiting their turn. This impulsivity can lead to social and academic challenges. You might have met such incidences in your journey. One of your friends would have been affected by such symptoms. As per the report of The World Health Organization (WHO) around 5% of children and 2.5% of adults worldwide have ADHD. This means that there are millions of people living with ADHD around the world.

However, these estimates can vary depending on the criteria used for diagnosis and the population studied. For example, in the United States, approximately 10.2% of children have been diagnosed with ADHD, according to a study published in JAMA Pediatrics in 2019.

It is important to note that ADHD is more commonly diagnosed in boys than girls, and in Black, non-Hispanic children than white children. But remember ADHD can affect anyone, regardless of age, race, or gender.

ADHD is thought to be a <u>neurodevelopmental disorder</u>. There are differences in the structure and function of certain brain regions, including the **prefrontal cortex,** which is involved in executive functions like attention, inhibition, and working memory. **Neurotransmitters** like dopamine and norepinephrine also play a role in regulating attention and impulse control, and imbalances in these neurotransmitters are associated with ADHD.

Diagnosis of ADHD typically involves a comprehensive assessment by a healthcare professional, including a review of the person's medical and developmental history, behavior observations, and the use of standardized rating scales. Treatment options often include behavioral interventions, psychoeducation, and medication. Stimulant medications like methylphenidate and amphetamines are commonly prescribed and can help improve focus and impulse control in many individuals with ADHD. However, the treating physician is the best judge of the situation to prescribe the proper medication.

ADHD can affect various aspects of life, including academic performance, work productivity, relationships, and self-esteem. However, with appropriate diagnosis and management, individuals with ADHD can learn strategies to cope with their symptoms and lead successful lives.

It's important to note that ADHD is a heterogeneous condition, meaning it can vary significantly in its presentation and impact from person to person. *ADHD*

. However, there are a variety of treatments available that can help people with ADHD to manage their symptoms and live full and productive lives.

Treatment for ADHD typically involves a combination of medication, therapy, and lifestyle changes. Medication can help to improve attention, focus, and impulse control. Therapy can help people with ADHD to develop coping skills and strategies for managing their symptoms. Lifestyle changes, such as getting regular exercise and eating a healthy diet, can also help to improve symptoms of ADHD.

With treatment, many people with ADHD are able to live successful and fulfilling lives. However, it is important to remember that ADHD is a lifelong condition. Symptoms may improve with age, but they are unlikely to completely disappear.

Early diagnosis and intervention, along with support from parents, teachers, and healthcare professionals, can greatly improve the outcomes for individuals with ADHD. On the other hand, improving attentional control can have beneficial effects on cognitive performance, emotional regulation, and stress management.

Selective Attention: How We Choose Which Stimuli to Attend to and Which to Ignore:

Selective attention is a cognitive process that allows individuals to focus their attention on relevant stimuli while ignoring irrelevant ones. It involves the ability to filter out distractions and prioritize the processing of specific sensory inputs.

"Attention is the rarest and purest form of generosity." - Simone Weil

It talks about the power of our attention. When we give someone our full attention, we are giving them the most precious gift we have. We are showing them that they are important to us and that we respect their time and thoughts. *In a world where we are constantly infused with distractions, it is more important than ever to learn the art of selective attention.*

Selective attention is necessary for many everyday tasks, such as driving, reading, and listening to a conversation in a noisy environment. It allows individuals to concentrate on important information and avoid being overwhelmed by irrelevant or distracting stimuli.

The process of selective attention involves several brain regions, including the frontal and parietal cortex, as well as subcortical structures such as the thalamus and basal ganglia. These regions work together to filter out irrelevant

sensory inputs and prioritize the processing of relevant information.

Several factors can influence selective attention, including motivation, emotion, and cognitive load. For example, individuals are more likely to attend to stimuli that are personally relevant or emotionally attached, and they may face more difficulty filtering out distractions when they are under a high cognitive load.

Deficits in selective attention can occur in a range of disorders, **including ADHD, schizophrenia, and traumatic brain injury**. On the other hand, training in selective attention can improve cognitive performance and academic achievement, particularly in children with ADHD.

Working Memory: How We Temporarily Hold and Manipulate Information in Our Minds while Completing Tasks:

Working memory is a cognitive system that allows individuals to temporarily hold and manipulate information in their minds while performing a task. It involves the processes of attention, encoding, maintenance, and retrieval of information.

"Working memory is a limited capacity system for temporarily storing and manipulating information that is essential for complex cognitive tasks." - Alan Baddeley

Working memory allows us to hold information in our minds while we are using it, such as when we are following a recipe, listening to directions, or doing a math problem. Working memory also plays a role in more complex tasks, such as planning, problem-solving, and reasoning. It also plays a pivotal role in learning, as it allows individuals to integrate new information with previously acquired knowledge.

Working memory is a limited resource, which means that we can only hold a certain amount of information in our minds at a time. This is why it is important to be selective about what information we focus on and to use strategies to help us manage our working memory load.

The human working memory system consists of several components, including the central executive, phonological loop, and visuospatial sketchpad. The central executive is responsible for controlling attention and coordinating the processing of information across different domains. **The phonological loop is involved in the temporary storage of verbal information, while the visuospatial sketchpad is responsible for holding visual and spatial information.**

Working memory capacity varies among individuals and is influenced by factors such as age, genetics, and training. Generally, working memory capacity declines with age, although training and practice can improve working memory performance. You can improve your working memory by following tips.

- Get enough sleep at least 7 hours during the night.

- Exercise regularly at least 5 days a week.

- Eat a healthy diet and avoid smoking, alcohol and drugs.

- Avoid distractions as practicable as it is.

- Break down complex tasks into smaller steps.

- Use mnemonic devices to remember information. (A mnemonic device is a learning technique that aids information retention or retrieval (remembering) in the human memory for better understanding. Mnemonic devices make use of elaborative encoding, retrieval cues, and imagery as specific tools to encode information in a way that allows for efficient storage and retrieval.) For example, the acrostic "My Very Educated Mother Just Served Us Nine Pizzas" can be used to remember the order of the planets in our solar system: Mercury, Venus, Earth, Mars, Jupiter, Saturn, Uranus, Neptune, and Pluto.

- Take breaks when you are working on a demanding task.

Deficits in working memory can occur in a range of disorders, including ADHD, schizophrenia, and Alzheimer's disease. On the other hand, training in working memory can improve cognitive performance and academic achievement, particularly in children with learning disabilities.

Cognitive Load:

"Cognitive load is the mental effort required to process information. Understanding and managing it is essential for effective teaching and learning." - John Sweller

Cognitive load refers to the amount of mental effort and resources required to complete a task or process information. It is a measure of the demand placed on an individual's working memory during a task.

There are three types of cognitive load: **intrinsic, extraneous, and germane.** Intrinsic cognitive load refers to the inherent complexity of the task itself, such as the number of steps involved or the level of difficulty. Extraneous cognitive load refers to the additional cognitive demands imposed by the task environment, such as distractions or irrelevant information. Germane cognitive load refers to the cognitive effort required to process and integrate information into long-term memory.

Cognitive load has a significant impact on learning and cognitive performance. High cognitive load can impair performance by taxing working memory, making it more difficult to retain and process information. On the other hand, optimal cognitive load can enhance performance by promoting learning and comprehension.

Several strategies can be used to manage cognitive load, such as breaking complex tasks into smaller, manageable chunks, providing clear and concise instructions, and reducing distractions in the task environment. Additionally, training in working memory can increase the capacity to handle cognitive load, improving overall cognitive performance.

Cognitive load is an essential concept in instructional design and educational psychology, as it can impact the effectiveness of teaching methods and materials. By understanding cognitive load, educators can design learning materials and instructional strategies that optimize learning and minimize cognitive overload.

Techniques such as brain imaging and cognitive testing can help researchers in this field gain a better understanding of how attention and focus work in the brain, as well as how they can be optimized for improved cognitive performance.

Chapter: 2

What are Distractions and Their Nature?

"The only way to avoid distractions is to completely disconnect from the world, and that's not realistic. The key is to learn to focus on what's important, even when there are distractions all around." – Unknown

Distraction refers to a state of mind where one's attention is diverted away from a primary task or focused toward something else. Distractions can come in various forms and can be either external or internal. Its magnitude may be small, large, or prolonged. Let's have a closer look at the nature of distraction:

1. External Distractions: These are distractions that originate from the environment or external stimuli. Common external distractions include the noise of industries, transport, loudspeakers, marketplace, notifications on electronic devices (such as smartphones or computers, televisions), people talking nearby, or any other sensory input that draws your attention away from what you're trying to concentrate on. It may also include any high-pitched exchange of words between two or more people as a sign of disagreement on any issue. Your family issues that disturb you are also a bigger external distraction. If not resolved in due time may become prolonged.

2. Internal Distractions: Internal distractions are thoughts, feelings, or mental processes that disrupt your focus. These can include daydreaming, worrying about personal issues, day-to-day concerns, or unrelated thoughts that wander through your mind while you're trying to focus on a task. The external distraction converts into internal issues. For example, in your business, you sustained a huge loss in the first quarter of a fiscal and you found the cause of the loss was not due to external factors but mismanagement by some of your employees. You will definitely be distracted by the outcome lose mental peace and take some drastic actions. You may also feel depressed about the happening. You may apprehend further loss if the situation and the management do not change. Every distraction originates externally but ruins you from within giving rise to anxiety, and depression. You can't anticipate any distractions but you become the victim of the circumstances. Without your knowledge, you are drawn to a controversy, a criminal incident, or similar happenings.

3. Multitasking: Attempting to do multiple tasks at the same time is called multitasking. While some people believe they are good at multitasking, it often leads to reduced efficiency and poorer task performance. In fact, multitasking keeps the brain in stress and the performer in a hurry. Someone unknown rightly says- **"Multitasking is like trying to cook three meals at once. You'll end up burning one, undercooking another, and the third will be mediocre."** Multitasking is a symbol of work overload and an act of distraction. It is not possible to undertake multiple tasks of an important nature. Monitoring post office tasks may be taken up in multitasking. Otherwise

"**Multitasking is a myth. What we're really doing is task switching, and it's actually making us less productive.**" - Gloria Mark

4. Digital Distractions: In the modern age, digital devices and the internet have introduced a whole new realm of distractions. Social media, email, text messages, and other online activities can constantly pull your attention away from your real task. Digital media not only draws your attention to unnecessary events it also kills your personal and professional life. Digital addiction destroys the very fabric of family life. When family life is disturbed, it is the end product of distractions.

5. Task-Specific Distractions: These are distractions that are directly related to the task at hand. For example, if you're studying and you come across a difficult concept, you might get distracted by trying to understand it, even if it's not the immediate topic you're supposed to be studying. Another example you are giving a presentation and thinking about what you're going to say next. At the same time Worrying about what the audience is thinking and checking the time.

6. Duration and Impact: Distractions can vary in duration and impact. Some distractions are momentary and easy to recover from, while others can be more prolonged and disrupt your workflow significantly. The impact of a distraction can range from a minor interruption to a complete loss of focus. For example, if you are a writer, your creativity depends on your concentration and thought process. During your writing flow, you hear somebody use slang language indicating you at your back or a child of your family cried loudly, it definitely distracts your writing. You may or may not concentrate on writing again after a few minutes.

7. Individual Variability: People have different levels of susceptibility to distractions. Some individuals may be highly sensitive to external stimuli, while others may have better concentration abilities. Personal factors like fatigue, stress, and cognitive load can also affect how distractions impact a person. Individual variability in distraction refers to the fact that different people may have varying levels of susceptibility to distractions based on their personality, cognitive traits, and environmental factors. For example- Introverts and extroverts may react differently to social distractions. Introverts tend to thrive in quieter, less stimulating environments and may find social interactions distracting. Extroverts, on the other hand, might be more inclined to seek social interaction and may not find it as distracting. So, in a shared workspace, an introverted individual may be more affected by nearby conversations, while an extroverted individual might be less bothered.

Strategies for Managing Distraction:

Managing distractions effectively is crucial for maintaining focus and productivity. You may follow some strategies to help you manage distractions. To get mental peace and a more productive environment you need to find a noise-free, quiet workspace. On many occasions, it is difficult to find such an environment and your desire may not be fulfilled. In such situations, you may use noise-canceling headphones and clearly define boundaries with others. Have a SMART goal before you that can give you intensity and focus. It has also proved on many occasions that when one is deeply engaged in a particular work is less prone to distractions.

Let me explain to you a tale of a mythical hero. You might have heard about the Indian mythical hero Arjun who found his name in the Indian great epic the Mahabharat and Bhagavad Gita. He aimed the eye of the revolving fish looking at its shadow in the water in a very chaotic and distracting environment of thousands present to get married to the princess of the Panchal kingdom Draupadi when all Pandavas were in exile. You mayn't understand the situation unless you see the issues empathetically. What made Arjun perform exceptionally well? The burning desire and intensity of achievement may be the right answer, as he has set the goal perfectly.

Pomodoro Technique can be used in your working space to avoid distractions and increase productivity. The Pomodoro Technique is a time management method that uses a timer to break down work into intervals, typically 25 minutes in length, separated by short breaks. This can help maintain concentration and provide scheduled times for distractions.

In the age of electronics and the internet, you can't find peace anywhere. You have to disable non-essential notifications like credit card offers, soaping mal offers, cricket scores, etc. on your smartphones and computers. This may reduce the temptation to check emails, social media, or other apps during focused work periods.

Prioritizing your Tasks can make you more focused and accountable even during noisy and distracting environments. You may find it easy to use techniques like the **Eisenhower Matrix** (quadrant method) to categorize tasks into four groups: _urgent and_

<u>important, important but not urgent, urgent but not important, and neither urgent nor important</u>. Focus on the most important and urgent tasks first. While prioritizing your task you must have a work schedule and the same must be shared with the people around you to be less affected by distraction. For example, you have a fixed daily schedule for Yoga at 7 P.M. All the people around you are aware that during your Yoga time, nobody can disturb you unless the most urgent task needs your intervention.

> ***"Multitasking is like trying to juggle three bowling balls. You can do it for a while, but eventually you're going to drop one."*** - James Clear, author of Atomic Habits

Multitasking may appear to work more but in fact, it does much damage to your efficiency and time management. However, single-tasking increases focus and efficiency giving rise to more production and fewer distractions. You may heard about some apps and browser extensions that can block distracting websites and apps. You may opt for the same for a specific time or forever to get rid of specific distractions. For example Freedom, Cold Turkey, leech Block NG, etc.

- *Freedom* is a popular distraction blocker that works on all of your devices, including computers, smartphones, and tablets. It allows you to block websites, apps, and even the entire internet for a specified period.

- *Cold Turkey Blocker* is another powerful distraction blocker that allows you to block websites, apps, and files. It also has a <u>"Forced Mode"</u> that prevents you from disabling the app or changing your settings.

- *Leech Block NG* is a free and open-source distraction blocker that works on most major browsers. It allows you to create lists of websites to block and then restrict them in all kinds of ways.

- *Rescue Time* is a time-tracking app that also has distraction-blocking features. You can use it to track how much time you spend on different websites and apps, and then block the most distracting ones.

- *Forest* is a gamified distraction blocker that helps you to stay focused by planting virtual trees. If you leave the app, your tree will die.

- *SelfControl* is a simple but effective distraction blocker for Mac OS X. It allows you to create a list of websites to block and then prevents you from accessing them for a specified period.

Moreover, you need to be organized in your workspace to complete the tasks in hand in due time. Procrastination can lead to future complications and distractions in completing the task to meet the dateline. Realistic expectations and setting goals may be viable to avoid distractions in the workspace. Further, your patience and capabilities to handle the awkward situation are key to settling all the issues in public or private life.

Above all **Mindfulness Exercises and Meditation** can help train your mind to stay focused and improve your ability to recognize and let go of distracting thoughts and manage situations and time effectively. <u>Because the inner piece is key to your success and accomplishment and you may not find peace outside your true self.</u>

Let me explain that not all distractions can be eliminated completely, but by implementing these strategies, you can significantly reduce their impact and improve your ability to stay focused on your tasks and goals. Experiment with different techniques to find what works best for you, as individual preferences and needs vary. There are various strategies for managing distractions, including time management techniques, creating a conducive work environment, setting boundaries with digital devices, practicing mindfulness, and using techniques like the Pomodoro Technique

The Benefits of Ignoring Distractions:

There are many benefits to ignoring distractions, both in terms of our productivity and our overall well-being. Some of the key benefits are as such;

1. **Improved Focus:** Distractions mean stress, anxiety, wastage of time, and mental agony. By ignoring distractions, we can improve our ability to focus on the task at hand. This can lead to increased productivity and better-quality work. Beyond distractions, we are free to dream, fly with wings and imagine. Today's dream is tomorrow's reality. Dr. APJ Abdul Kalam, the former President of India and a renowned scientist, was known for his inspirational quotes on dreams and vision. He says; **"Dream, dream, dream. Dreams transform into thoughts and thoughts result in action."** A dream is the first step of your action and the flower of your thought process. Unless you

dream, you may not imagine big and may not proceed ahead in your journey to your destination.

2. **Reduced Stress**: Distractions can cause stress and anxiety. In many cases, it is observed that the distractions ruin lives. Especially when we feel like we are not able to accomplish what we need to because of them. By ignoring distractions, we can reduce these negative emotions and feel more in control of our work and our lives.

3. **Better Decision-Making:** When we can focus on the most important information, we can make better decisions. When you make any decisions out of the impact of distraction, it has every chance to backfire. Ignoring distractions allows us to prioritize what matters most and make more informed choices making our lives easy and comfortable.

4. **Increased Creativity:** When we are not constantly interrupted by distractions, we can allow our minds to concentrate and come up with new ideas. Ignoring distractions can lead to increased creativity and innovation. Especially when you are in creative writing, distraction causes huge damage to the creation process. Being a writer I can say with authority that the same thoughts and powerful feelings of the moment may not be repeated later.

5. **Improved Relationships:** Ignoring distractions, improves relationships in the manifold. No distractions means we are more focused and present in the moment and engaged in our relationships with others. This can lead to

better communication, deeper connections, and more fulfilling relationships.

Overall, ignoring distractions can have a powerful impact on our ability as a human being. It helps us to accomplish our goals, reduce stress, and improve our overall well-being.

Chapter: 3

Overcoming Information Overload

What is Information Overload?

Information overload is a situation faced by an individual to make an informed decision when he has too much information about that issue. It generally happens when an excessive quantity of daily information is received. The overlapping information creates confusion in the mind of an individual making him what to do first.

In the 21st century, we are pressed with information from all sides. We have access to more information than ever before. It is due to the internet and other digital technologies. However, this influx of information can be overwhelming. It can be difficult to know what information is relevant and important, and what information can be ignored. For examples;

- Checking your email inbox multiple times an hour, even when you're off the clock.

- Having a social media feed that is constantly scrolling with new updates.

- Watching TV while listening to music and checking your phone.

Information overload can lead to several negative impacts including:

- **Stress and anxiety:** It is the curse of modern-day living. When we try to process too much information at our fingertips can be stressful and provoke anxiety.

- **Poor decision-making:** When we have too much information, we may not be able to process them correctly which can lead to ineffective decisions. Such decisions are based on incomplete or inaccurate information.

- **Reduced productivity:** Information overload can lead to reduced productivity, as we spend more time trying to manage information. Time can't be extended for us doing actually get work done.

- **Burnout:** Information overload can lead to a complicated situation like burnout in us. It is a state of physical, emotional, and mental fatigue.

It is important to manage information overload to survive and enjoy a healthy lifestyle.

Learning to Filter Out What Doesn't Matter:

Learning to filter out what doesn't matter is an important skill in today's information-rich world. With so much information available at our fingertips, it can be difficult to discern what is truly important and what is not. In a multitasking environment, filtering out irrelevant information is more relevant for better management of time and opportunities. You have to make some strategies to keep yourself updated and avoid distractions.

Prioritize all your tasks. Make a list of the most important tasks and goals you need to accomplish, and focus on those first. Note down them serially on priority. This will help you avoid getting sidetracked by less important tasks and distractions. Establish boundaries around your time and attention. This might mean turning off notifications on your phone or email or setting aside specific times of day to check them. Specific time slots for specific tasks be earmarked. For example Yoga and meditation time in the evening from 7 PM to 8 PM. For the specific task switch off your mobile, to keep you out of distractions. You can use filters to sort through your email and other online communication. This can help you quickly identify what is important and what can be deleted or ignored. Further, you have to develop a system for organizing and managing information. This might include a to-do list, a calendar, or a project management tool.

Practice Mindfulness can help you to a big extent to help you stay focused and present in the moment. This can help you avoid getting caught up in distractions and stay focused on what truly matters. If you practice mindfulness meditation regularly you may not be disturbed or hugely disappointed by any distractions in your home or office or in public life. It is a practical tip practiced by many successful people around the world.
Let me explain a small incident in the life of Mahatma Gandhi, the father of the nation (India). In pre-independent India Gandhijee was busy uniting the freedom fighters to fight against foreign rule (British) in

a non-violent way and was in constant touch with Britons engaging in meetings and discussions. He has also developed a good relationship with some offices of alien rulers and some take him as their adversary. One day an officer wrote Gandhijee a letter with derogative narratives about him and sent it through a messenger. The messenger was instructed to fix the letter on the wall of Gandhi's residence in the forenoon with an iron barb. The instruction was carried out.

On the day of the incident, a meeting of Gandhijee was scheduled with British officers in the afternoon. Gandhijee attended the scheduled meeting. Interestingly the said officer, who has written the letter was also present in the meeting. He was expecting some sort of disappointment from Gandhijee but in vain. After the meeting was over out of excitement the said offer asked "<u>Have not you got my letter?</u>" Gandhijee replied in affirmation making the Briton surprised. Further, he said "<u>I have read your letter but was not useful for me and not accepted to my heart. But I collected the iron barb found useful for me.</u>"

Gandhijee made a very informed decision to keep distraction (the derogatory language and contents) at bay. That kept him fresh without coming under any mental pressure. **It is a learning for all of us to focus on the things that matter to us not the unnecessary burden.**

In daily life, small matters having meaningless content distract us. Because we fail to filter the same at the very moment because of our reactive tendencies. However, it is not a general inference but human-specific. The same incident may be filtered by two individuals separately. Filtering the right information matter most.

Techniques for Prioritizing Information:

Prioritizing information is essential to manage information overload and ensure you focus on what is most important. First, set clear goals and objectives to help you determine what information is most relevant to your needs. Categorizing information is the second step based on its importance and relevance to your goals. This might include categorizing information by urgency, level of importance, or type of information.

You may opt for a ranking system to prioritize information based on its level of importance. This might include assigning a numerical value or a color code to different types of information. You may follow the following ranking system for strategies to overcome information overload, from most effective to least effective:

- *Prioritize information:* Focus on the most important information and filter out the rest. Prioritize information that is relevant, important, and immediately urgent and needs immediate attention.

- *Limit distractions:* Minimize distractions, such as notifications, emails, or phone calls that can disrupt focus and attention. Set aside dedicated time for specific tasks, and avoid multitasking. The distractions can include any noise of the construction works, the noise of the marketplaces, loud voices, and derogatory remarks about you or your actions. Some accusations by your boss or authority or colleagues. Any third-party intervention in your family matters or love life. Unpleasant incidents in the workspace are other distractions that are more damaging to your reputation and mental peace. You have to manage it with clear vision and authority.

- _Use technology tools_: Utilize technology tools such as filtering software, bookmarking apps, and productivity tools to help manage and organize information.

- _Practice mindfulness:_ Mindfulness practices, such as meditation, can help reduce stress and increase focus, leading to improved information processing.

- _Take breaks:_ Regular breaks can help alleviate mental fatigue and improve cognitive performance. Take short breaks between tasks or longer breaks during extended periods of work. In fact, breaks repair the illness of the body and mind reducing stress and overcoming anxieties.

- _Develop time management skills:_ Effective time management skills can help allocate time to tasks more efficiently, reducing the feeling of being overwhelmed by information. Time is a big factor in human activities. Time and tide wait for none. It can go at its usual speed and you can't bank it but spend it intelligently.

- _Get enough sleep:_ Is not funny to advise someone to get enough sleep, when he is in distress or under tremendous pressure? How can one get sound sleep with anxiety? Yes, it is right. Do you think one can live in distress or anxiety forever? No, you have to overcome the same for which adequate sleep is crucial for cognitive functioning, including attention, memory, and decision-making. Lack of sleep can impair cognitive performance and increase the feeling of information overload. It also leads to many health hazards.

- *Seek Expert Advice:* Intelligent people are around you. They are called experts or life coaches. You may also seek expert advice to help you determine what information is most important and relevant to your needs if you fail to sort out the issues. This might include consulting with a mentor or subject matter expert.

It's important to note that these strategies or suggestions may not work equally for everyone, and they may require a combination of approaches to overcome information overload effectively. However, by prioritizing information, you can make more informed decisions, stay focused on what is most important, and avoid getting overwhelmed by the amount of information available.

Chapter: 4

The Role of Mindfulness in Ignoring Distractions

The Power of Mindfulness for Finding Focus:

"Mindfulness is the energy of being fully present. When we're mindful, we're not caught up in the thoughts of the past or the future. We're not judging or criticizing ourselves or others. We're simply aware of the present moment." - Tara Brach

Mindfulness is a mental state achieved by focusing one's awareness on the present moment. It is a moment to calmly acknowledge and accept one's feelings, thoughts, and bodily sensations. It has become increasingly popular in recent years as a way to improve mental health, reduce stress and anxiety, and increase overall well-being.

One of the key benefits of mindfulness is its ability to help individuals find focus. When the mind is concentrated to a particular point and focused on the task at hand, mindfulness can help individuals achieve greater levels of productivity and efficiency. Some key parameters of the mindfulness are observed as follows;

1. **It trains the mind to be present:** Mindfulness helps individuals become more aware of their thoughts and feelings in the present moment, rather than dwelling on the past or worrying about the future. It is a regular training to the mind to stay present, individuals are better able to focus on the task at hand. Because the mind is fickle and it wonders. One may find it difficult to control it. It requires regular practice and consistency to train the mind. In Bhagavad Gita Krishna answers a query from his devoted friend Arjun. (Chapter 2, Verse 72.)

असंशयं महाबाहो मनो दुर्निग्रहं चलम्।

अभ्यासेन तु कौन्तेय वैराग्येण च गृह्यते।।

asaṁśayaṁ mahā-bāho mano durnigrahaṁ calam

abhyāsena tu kaunteya vairāgyeṇa ca gṛhyate

In His address, Lord Krishna says- undoubtedly, the mind is restless and difficult to control. However, it can be brought under control through practice and detachment. Here the word practice means mindfulness practice like Yoga. Gradual and regular practice of Yoga prepares the mind to concentrate on the present and detach negative qualities.

2. **It reduces distractions**: Distraction is the principal enemy of the people of all of us in this era of technology. Technology no doubt made us advanced and knowledgeable but also stole our mental peace. It is the principal source of distraction. Mindfulness helps individuals become more aware of their surroundings and the distractions that may be present. Recognizing these distractions is necessary to eradicate them. Once it is detected the individuals can more easily tune them out and focus on the task at hand.

3. **It improves concentration**:
    "The secret of accomplishment is concentration or the art of turning all your power upon just one point at a time." - Swami Vivekananda
    When you concentrate on a single point or agenda, you are more accomplished to complete it with full satisfaction. Mindfulness provides positive energy and the intention to focus on the task without distraction. This helps individuals improve their ability to concentrate on the work at hand for an extended period of time.

4. **It enhances creativity**: Every individual is unique and creative in his mind. However, creativity is not nurtured by everybody due to different factors including socio-cultural and economic factors. Distraction and improper training are other factors responsible for the lack of creativity. When you find the technique and temperament to overcome the same you are more productive in actions. Mindfulness makes you present and fully engaged in the task at hand, and likely to tap into your creative abilities and come up with new and innovative ideas.

Mindfulness is a powerful tool for finding focus. A trained mind can be present, at the moment, reducing distractions, improving concentration, and enhancing creativity, individuals can achieve greater levels of productivity and efficiency in their daily lives.

Techniques for Practicing Mindfulness:

Practicing mindfulness is a powerful way to improve mental health, reduce stress and anxiety, and increase overall well-being. In the present era of distraction practicing mindfulness is the utmost priority for success and keeping depression and anxiety-like conditions at bay. You may practice the following few techniques for practicing mindfulness:

Mindful Breathing:

Mindful breathing is a simple but powerful practice that can help you reduce stress, improve focus, and increase self-awareness. It is simply the act of paying attention to your breath, without trying to change it in any way.

To practice mindful breathing, find a quiet place where you will not be disturbed. Sit in a comfortable position, either with your back straight or lying down. Close your eyes or lower your gaze, and focus your attention on your breath.

Notice the rise and fall of your chest as you breathe in and out. Pay attention to the sensation of air entering and leaving your nostrils. You may also notice the movement of your belly as you breathe. Don't try to change your breath in any way. Simply observe it, without judgment. If your mind wanders, gently bring it back to your breath. It is normal for your mind to wander, especially when you are first starting. Don't get discouraged. Just gently bring your attention back to your breath.

You can start by practicing mindful breathing for a few minutes at a time. As you become more comfortable, you can gradually increase the amount of time you practice.

You can practice mindful breathing at any time of day, but it is especially helpful to do it in the evening or morning. Fix specific time slots for the purpose. You may practice the same when you are angry, feeling stressed, or anxious. You can also use mindful breath to help you to focus and concentrate.

Body Scan Meditation:

Body scan meditation is a form of mindfulness meditation that involves bringing your attention to different parts of your body in a systematic manner. It can be a helpful way to reduce stress, improve body awareness, and promote relaxation.

For performing body scan meditation, find a quiet place without external interference or distraction. Lie down on your back in a comfortable position, with both your eyes closed. Place your hands on your belly or chest, as you find comfortable, and take a few deep breaths.

Once you feel settled, begin to bring your attention to your toes. Notice any sensations you are feeling, such as warmth, coolness, pressure, or tension. If you don't feel any sensations, that's okay too. Simply observe without judgment. After a few moments, bring your attention to your calves, and then to your thighs. Continue scanning your body in this way, moving up to your hips, abdomen, chest, shoulders, arms, neck, and head. As you scan each part of your body, simply observe any sensations you are feeling, without thinking further. If your mind wanders, gently bring it back to your breath.

Continue scanning your body until you reach the top of your head. Once you have scanned your entire body, take a few deep breaths and rest in silence for a few minutes. You can do a body scan meditation for as long or as short as you like. A good starting point is 10-15 minutes. As you become more comfortable with the practice, you can gradually increase the time span.

Body scan meditation is a very simple process but needs patience. It can be a helpful practice for people of all ages and abilities. It can help individuals become more aware of their physical sensations and develop a deeper connection with their bodies and mind.

Mindful Walking:

Mindful walking is a combination of physical exercise and mindfulness. It is a simple but effective way to reduce stress, improve mood, and increase self-awareness. It also needs a quiet place for walking. Take a few deep breaths to calm your mind and body. Then, begin walking at a slow, comfortable pace. As you walk, pay attention to the sensations of your feet touching the ground. Notice the movement of your legs and the rhythm of your breath. Be aware of the sights, sounds, and smells around you.

If your mind starts to wander, gently bring it back to your breath or the sensations of your feet touching the ground. Don't judge yourself if your mind wanders. It is normal for the mind to wander, especially when you are first starting out. You can practice mindful walking for 10-15 minutes in the initial days. As you become more comfortable with the practice, you can gradually increase the time for your walk. You can prefer the morning or evening for the above task.

Mindful walking is a simple but powerful practice that can have a significant impact on your physical, mental, and overall well-being. It is a great way to reduce stress, improve mood, increase self-awareness, and cultivate a sense of calm and peace.

Mindful Eating:

This technique involves paying attention to the sensory experience of eating, including the taste, smell, and texture of the food. By slowing down and savoring each bite, individuals can develop a deeper appreciation for food and a more mindful approach to eating. Mindful eating is a skill that takes time and practice to develop.

But even a little bit of mindful eating can make a difference in your overall health and well-being.

Mindful Visualization:

Mindful visualization is a type of meditation that involves using your imagination to create and experience positive images and scenes. It can be used to reduce stress, improve mood, boost creativity, and crush goals.

An isolated and quiet place is suitable for such practice. Sit or lie down in a comfortable position. Close your eyes and take a few deep breaths to relax your body and mind. Once you feel relaxed, begin to visualize a positive image or scene. It could be a place you love to be, a person you care about, or an activity you enjoy doing.

Use all of your senses to create the image or scene in your mind. What do you see? What do you hear? What do you smell? What do you feel? The more vivid and detailed your visualization, the more effective it will be. Your mind may wander, but nothing to worry about. It is a normal behavior of the mind and gently bring it back to your visualization. Don't judge yourself if your mind wanders. Continue visualizing for as long as possible. You may start it with 5 minutes a day preferably evening or morning. When you finish the task, take a few deep breaths and open your eyes.

Overall, there are many techniques for practicing mindfulness, and individuals may find that certain techniques work better for them than others. The key is to find a technique that resonates with you and to make mindfulness a regular part of your daily routine. Remember when you are going to practice mindfulness, leave the distracting elements like mobiles, and electronic devices back.

Mindfulness and the Art of Ignoring Distractions:

Distractions are a common obstacle to mindfulness practice. The distractions may be technological, environmental, personal, social, external, etc in different forms and magnitudes. But you have to identify the nature of the distractions for redressal. Unless you are aware of the actual forms of the distraction you can't find the solution. However, once you identify the culprit with consistent effort and practice, can learn to ignore distractions and stay focused on the present moment. You may follow some tips for cultivating the art of ignoring distractions:

Acknowledge the distraction: When a distraction arises, don't try to ignore it or push it away. Instead, acknowledge its presence and simply let it be. Recognize that distractions are a natural part of the human experience and that it's okay to be distracted from time to time. Unless you admit the distraction as part of the modern-day lifestyle, you may not ignore it easily. In fact, nothing to take into heart. For example, one election rally is passing through your lane in the early evening during your meditation time. What to do then? Nothing but to watch or close your doors and windows. Never lose your temper that may disturb you more. The only solution left for you is to wait for the noise to pass your lane and calm down.

Label the distraction: To label a distraction, simply identify it and name it. For example, if you are working on a project and you find yourself checking your email every few minutes, you can label that distraction "email checking." You may broadly divide distractions into two categories, such as external and internal distractions. Name external distractions such as Noise: "traffic noise", Other people: "coworkers talking", and Physical discomfort: "hunger". In the same manner, you may name, Internal distractions: Daydreaming: "Daydreaming about vacation". Worrying: "worrying about tomorrow's presentation", ruminating on negative thoughts: "Thinking about that argument I had with my friend". There is no specific formula to do the same, you may name it at your convenience.

Once you have labeled your distraction, you can start to develop strategies for dealing with it. For example, if you are distracted by email checking, you can try turning off your email notifications or setting aside a specific time each day to check your email. Labeling distractions can be helpful because it allows you to become more aware of them. It can also help you to identify patterns in your distractions. For example, you may notice that you are more likely to be distracted by email in the afternoon or that you are more likely to daydream when you are feeling stressed. Once you are aware of your distractions and their patterns, you can start to develop more effective strategies for managing them.

Practice regularly: Like any skill, the art of ignoring distractions takes practice. Make mindfulness a regular part of your daily routine, and be patient with yourself as you learn to stay focused in the face of distractions.

Be kind to yourself: Remember you are your best friend and have to love you most. Mindfulness is a practice, and there's no such thing as a perfect practice. If you do become distracted, don't beat yourself up about it, and never give up. Simply acknowledge the distraction, label it, and refocus your attention on the present moment.

Overall, the art of ignoring distractions is an essential part of mindfulness practice. By acknowledging distractions, labeling them, and refocusing on the present moment, individuals can cultivate greater levels of focus, concentration, and peace of mind. It only depends on your burning desire to get success on the path to mindfulness. Once you decide means turn it into action. When you start taking action everything will be settled systematically and never doubt your ability to excel.

Chapter: 5

Balancing Attention and Obligation

The Fine Line between Ignoring and Neglecting:

"Ignoring and neglecting others are the two biggest mistakes we can make in life. They are the root of all conflict and pain." - Unknown

The fine line between ignoring and neglecting can be difficult to navigate. Ignoring someone or something can be a deliberate choice to not engage or respond to them, whereas neglecting implies a lack of care or attention. In both cases, the neglected and ignored are punished with or without their fault.

In some cases, ignoring can be an appropriate choice and response, such as when dealing with a toxic or abusive person. Ignoring their behavior can be a way to protect oneself and set boundaries. However, ignoring someone who badly needs your help or support can be neglectful and harmful.

Examples of some situations where you cannot ignore;

- In parenting, it is your sacred duty to attend to the feelings of your children. In no circumstances you should ignore their sentiments and feelings. For example, your child is rigid in asking for a toy in a departmental store, but you can't afford it, in that situation, you have to convince and divert your child's attention to another affordable toy.

- You may not ignore traffic rules. Ignoring the rules means an offense leads to financial loss and risk of cancellation of driver's license.

- Your friend is in dire need of money and came begging for one thousand dollars and you have enough money. You may not ignore his presence or his situation. Consider his problem empathetically.

Examples of situations where you can ignore.

- You are presenting a project report and a few rude comments strike you but you turn a deaf ear and proceed with the presentation. But you can't ignore answering the query.

- When encountering offensive or hurtful comments on social media or the internet, you should choose to ignore the trolls rather than engage in an argument or give them the attention they seek.

- In a busy work environment, it's often necessary to ignore minor distractions like background noise or non-essential notifications to stay focused on important tasks.

- When you receive overly harsh or unjustified criticism, it can be beneficial to ignore it, especially if it's not constructive and is only intended to bring you down.

- In personal relationships, there may be times when it's better to ignore minor disagreements or petty arguments rather than escalate the conflict and cause unnecessary tension.

  However, it's important to note that ignoring situations should be done judiciously. Some issues may warrant addressing or resolving rather than ignoring, depending on their significance and potential impact.

Neglecting someone or something is a failure to provide the necessary care or attention. It can result in harm or negative consequences. Neglect can occur in various forms, such as neglecting a child's emotional or physical needs, neglecting a relationship, or neglecting responsibilities at work.

Some examples of neglect in various contexts:

1. A child has every right to get love, affection, and care from his parents and family. You are a parent and not giving any attention to providing your child with the

necessary basic needs for food, clothing, shelter, or medical care.

2. Every elderly parent has every right to get respect and care from their children. If their needs such as medicines, food, shelter, and respect are not met. Further, they are neglected particularly in nursing homes or caregiving situations, by not providing proper care, attention, or assistance.

3. _Neglecting self is the biggest example of neglect._ When an individual neglects their own physical or mental health, hygiene, or well-being, often due to underlying issues like depression, addiction, carelessness, or other mental health disorders whatever the issue may be.

4. The disregard for the environment by not taking steps to reduce pollution, conserve resources, or address environmental problems, contributing to issues like pollution and climate change.

5. Within a business or organization, neglect can refer to a lack of attention or investment in areas such as employee development, safety measures, or maintaining equipment, which can lead to various problems or inefficiencies. Non-performance of duty in the organization.

These examples illustrate different forms of neglect, all of which can have significant consequences and should be addressed and prevented whenever possible.

It is important to understand the difference between ignoring and neglecting, as well as the potential consequences of both. Ignoring can be a tool for self-protection, but it should not be used to avoid responsibilities or obligations. Neglecting can have serious consequences and should be addressed promptly.

Strategies for Balancing Attention and Obligation:

"The key to work-life balance is not to eliminate either work or life. It is to learn to live each one to the fullest." - Jeffrey Gitomer

Everybody has priorities and obligations on this earth. You may not be so selfish for non-obligation. Nobody can escape this truth anyway. This obligation may have many wings such as toward the profession, family, loved one, and self. You may not neglect any one of the above, but have to manage tactfully and efficiently. Do you love your job or profession only? Do you give more attention to your job than your parents, wife, and children? Many have different answers to these questions. Somebody says yes love my job for my family. Yes, he is absolutely right. Job is the source of money and earnings. Money is the utmost necessity to run the family. But can you afford to neglect your family, parents, and children for the job? Absolutely not. I feel neglecting your old parents for your family or job is an injustice to god and humanity. Do you remember the sacrifice they have made for you? Unless you are parent can't understand the same. Then you are in a dilemma in getting the solutions to your problems. Yes, you might have heard, that every problem has a solution. You have to perform the acts of balancing attention and obligation.

Make a list of your obligations and prioritize them based on their importance and urgency. You may not compromise with your duty. It is a fine and praiseworthy mindset. But at the same time for the sake of work, you mayn't befool your family. After office hours, attend to your family, and old parent. Never feel overwhelmed by the responsibilities you shoulder. When you prioritize your tasks, it can help you focus your attention on the most important tasks and avoid feeling guilty.

Your time and energy are limited in the first changing world. You have to establish boundaries around your time and energy. Learn to say no to obligations that are not necessary or that you do not have the capacity for. It is often difficult to say no to near and dear but you have to opt for unnecessary obligation.

For example, you have planned for a foreign trip with family on your next vacation but your old parent fell ill suddenly with multiple complications and was admitted to hospital. Now what option is left with you? Should you proceed with your plan or postpone it? I know that you are responsible enough to postpone or cancel your tour. Because your presence is more precious to them than any other matter on the earth. You may not like to lose them or be left unattended to suffer. Here your mental support is more necessary than financial support. Both may be required if your parent has not saved enough for the old age care.

Time management is a big skill and a symbol of sincerity. Develop good time management skills by scheduling your day and allocating specific times for work, rest, and other activities. This can help you stay on track and avoid wasting time. You should not forget

"Your greatest asset is your earning ability. Your greatest resource is your time." - Jim Rohn. You can't waste time gossiping or unproductive uses. Moreover spending time in bad company is harmful to you as well as to your family and society. You are the best resource for you and the best adviser for yourself. You may also like to delegate some tasks to others to reduce workload and to take up more important assignments and obligations. **This can also help others develop new skills and take on more responsibilities. Remember one-man army may not get victory on every front and occasion.**

Love yourself more than your loved one. You are the most valued individual for yourself when self-care and self-love come for discussion. Make sure to take care of your physical, mental, and emotional health. Be obliged to yourself first. This includes getting enough rest, eating healthy diets, doing regular exercise, and engaging in activities that bring you joy and feel relaxed. You can perform more obligations when you are fine and full of positive energy. When a pot is full of water, it can quench the thirst of many. The human body and mind behave like that. Self-care is like filling the pot with pure water. Eleanor Brownn righty says-*"**Self-care is not selfish. You cannot serve from an empty vessel.**"* It is the miracle of self-care that most neglects. Love yourself to give more, produce more, empower more, and enhance more.

Moreover, when completing obligations, focus on the quality of your work rather than the quantity. This can help you avoid burnout and maintain a healthy balance between your attention and obligations.

However, finding a balance between attention and obligation is an ongoing process. It takes time, effort, and practice to develop effective strategies and maintain a healthy balance. When you are mentally prepared to perform, means you are a warrior and have the intensity and intention to perform.

Tips for Setting Boundaries and Prioritizing Your Time:

Setting boundaries and prioritizing your time both are important but can be challenging. However, it's essential to maintain your well-being and achieve your goals. Here are some tips to help you:

- Everybody has some priorities that may be small or big. A man without priorities is simply a living being without any planning for his future or a saint of any expectation. It may happen that he has lost any hope in his future. But being a human of perfect knowledge and wit you have to prioritize your task first. Take some time to reflect on what's important to you and what you want to achieve. Write down your priorities serially to focus on your goals and values to help you stay focused on what really matters.

- During your performances on the journey to goals, you may face many complications, hardships, and harassment. Some situations might have arisen that have made you down. All such situations may have been averted only by saying the simple word "no". *Simple and timid people always suffer in our societies due to a lack of self-awareness. Saying no can be hard, but it's important to set limits on what you can and cannot do. Be realistic and assertive about your approach. Never think about other's perception of you when you say no or turn down their request.* However, be polite when saying no, and don't feel guilty for prioritizing your time and energy.

- You have to create a schedule to get your work done and dreams are fulfilled. Unless you create a schedule you may face difficulties in monitoring your tasks at hand. It can help you manage your time more effectively. Plan out your day or week, including time for work, leisure, and self-care. It may be better for you to use tools to help you stay organized. So many apps and tools can help you stay organized, and motivated such as a to-do list, a calendar, or a productivity app. Find what works best for you and use it consistently. When you are prioritizing your tasks, learn to delegate some work to the trusted. You don't have to do everything yourself. Self-care is essential to maintaining your well-being and avoiding burnout as discussed earlier. Make time for activities that bring you joy and relaxation, such as exercise, meditation, or hobbies.

- Life is beautiful when you are flexible in your approach and applications. Life is unpredictable, and things may not always go according to plan. Be flexible and willing to adjust your priorities and boundaries as needed.

In fact, life is a great teacher, and life experiences teach us to manage the affairs of life tactfully. Remember time is a great leveler, and you have to march forward managing time effectively.

Remember, setting boundaries and prioritizing your time takes practice and consistency. But with time and effort, you can find a balance that works for you and helps you achieve your goals while maintaining your well-being.

Chapter: 6

Cultivate a Positive Mindset

The Impact of Negative Thoughts and Self-Talk:

"The words we tell ourselves have a powerful impact on our lives. If we constantly put ourselves down, we're going to have a hard time achieving our goals." - Louise Hay

Negative thoughts and self-talk can have a profound impact on our mental and physical health, as well as our overall well-being. When we engage in negative self-talk, we create a negative internal dialogue that can affect our emotions, behavior, and relationships with others. The origin of self-talk is our failure in some tasks or actions. When we want immediate and instant results without waiting for the minimum gestation period, we are occasionally affected by negative self-talk. Another issue in negative self-talk and negative thoughts is a lack of self-confidence. When you are unaware of your worthiness and self-power then you are easily a victim of negativity. Remember you are a unique creation of the almighty and you are made for a specific purpose not to be discouraged by temporary setbacks. You are well acquainted with the fact that nothing in this mortal world is permanent. Both good and bad, happiness and unhappiness, success and failure are relative terms and have no permanent existence. If you are at present on the back foot don't worry you will be on the front foot very soon. Have patience.

You might have heard the fable of a tortoise and a rabbit and their race to reach a destination. Let me explain the same in a few sentences. Once both a rabbit and a tortoise decided to run for a distance in a certain course. Both started running at the same time. The rabbit ran fast covered many distance and looked back, the tortoise was nowhere near him. Now he decided to take a rest under a tree and get sleep. When he raised and ran to the destination to his surprise tortoise crossed the winning line by the time he reached. Now what is the message from the fable we got? Not to be overwhelmed by any task or any circumstances and be consistence in our assigned duties or actions. If the tortoise is overwhelmed by seeing his competitor he might not have agreed to the race. However, the tortoise proved that "slow and steady wins the race". Be optimistic in your approach and attitude and be consistence in your performance. It is natural that negativity can come to your mind but can't disturb you anymore.

Some of the effects of negative thoughts and self-talk include:

1. **Decreased Self-esteem:** Negative self-talk can erode our self-esteem and make us feel unworthy, unlovable, and incompetent. When you cut your tongue, no one can stop your

action. Because you are your first guardian. You are your best friend and adviser. If your best and loving one underestimates you and stabs at back then to whom you will believe? Decreased self-esteem means you are left nowhere. Lysa TerKeurst an American speaker, a bestselling author says- **"Negative self-talk is like a poison that we drink ourselves."** How can you survive for how many days drinking poison? Remember when you are at a disadvantage everybody will like to settle their score against you. But you have nothing to react to but to wait for the opportunity to retaliate.

2. **Increased Anxiety and Depression:** Negative thoughts can trigger anxiety and depression, which can weaken you both physically and mentally. Because both physical and mental health are reciprocal and interconnected to each other. Your mind is the leader of your body. When your mind is disturbed and unhealthy it is most likely to damage your physical health. You may lose good sleep and your body functions may be affected adversely leading to a range of physical symptoms such as fatigue, insomnia, and loss of appetite.

3. **Poor Coping Skills**: Negative self-talk can make it difficult to cope with stress and adversity, leading to unhealthy behaviors. Behavior is a benchmark of your personality. When you are affected by negative self-talk you may not have the courage and vitality to perform your task as usual and face the others. You may

develop irritation, anger, fear, and rigidity. Further, you may love isolation, and loneliness and may like sad songs.

4. **Relationship Problems**: Negative self-talk can create a negative cycle that can impact our relationships with others. It can lead us to become defensive, critical, and withdrawn, making it difficult to form and maintain healthy relationships. When you are driven by sadness may not like others in happiness. Because it is the law of nature. Rachel Boston an American actress says rightly-"**Negative self-talk is like wearing a pair of sunglasses that only let you see the bad in everything. Take them off and see the world for the beautiful place it is.**"

5. **Physical Health Problems:** Research has shown that negative thoughts and self-talk can impact our physical health, leading to chronic conditions such as heart disease, diabetes, and chronic pain. It is said, "Health is wealth". You may not afford to lose such a god-gifted wealth with negative feelings and self-talk. When you are not aware of yourself, such a complication arises.

However, you may not live in negativity forever to destroy yourself. You have to get out of the temporary setbacks leading to negative self-talk. It is important to identify and challenge negative thoughts and self-talk in order to promote positive mental health. You can apply some time-tested practices such as mindfulness, cognitive behavioral therapy, and positive affirmations, among others to make your inner self happy for overall wellbeing.

Techniques for Ignoring Negative Thoughts and Self-Talk:

Keep in your mind that you are the best master and guide of yourself. You have to ignore the negative sensations being raised out of negative self-talk and thoughts. Ignoring negative thoughts and self-talk can be challenging, but not out of your capacity and capabilities. Several techniques have been developed that can help you to come out of the clutches of negativity. Here are some time-tested strategies you can use to manage negative self-talk:

Mindfulness:

Mindfulness is one of the best practices you can follow to get rid of mental agony. It involves focusing on the present moment and being aware of your thoughts and feelings without judgment. When you notice negative self-talk, try to observe it non-judgmentally and let it pass without reacting to it. When you react more to any situation or incident you attract the situation more. In mindfulness meditation, you just let the negative thoughts come and go and don't make any judgments. Be present in the moment as a mute spectator. Remember nobody has ever seen the future as reality only focusing on the present can help you to marginalize negativity. Amit Ray an Indian author, philosopher, spiritual master, and pioneer of the Compassionate AI movement rightly says-**"If you want to conquer the** anxiety of life, live in the moment, and live in the breath."

Positive Affirmations:

Positive affirmation is like an ignition to your mental engine which is running on back gear to make toward forward motion.

For example,

- If your negative thought is **"I am not worthy of love"**
- Its counter-positive affirmation shall be **"I am worthy of love as I am handsome or talented."**

If you are disappointed in getting a suitable job for you and the negative thoughts like

- **"I am not fit for getting my dream job"**, that can be countered by positive affirmations like
- **"I am talented and worthy of getting my dream job (job name)**.

You prepare your positive affirmation as per your requirements and repeat it as much you like with your full emotion anytime you like. Fit it in autopilot mode to get quick results. If you repeat it before retiring to bed and just after leaving the bed early morning, it can do magic. However, remember you have every potential to turn the negativity into positive emotion to get better results. Affirmations can help counteract negative self-talk and promote a more positive outlook.

Reframing Thought Patterns:

Reframing thought patterns is another way to lead you on a positive path. Reframing involves taking a negative thought or belief and rephrasing it more positively or

realistically. Some examples are for better understanding;

- If you think "I'm never going to succeed, in getting my executive job at Google" you can reframe it as "I may face challenges, but I have the skills and resources to overcome them to get my dream job at Google."
- If you think "I'm not handsome enough to have a beautiful girl as a life partner" you can reframe it as "I am handsome externally and have inner beauty and am talented enough to attract a beautiful girl to my life as a life partner."

Cognitive Restructuring:

Cognitive restructuring is a very powerful tool involved in addressing the negative thought pattern and its restructuring. Here you just identify and challenge negative thoughts and beliefs by examining the evidence for and against them. For example, **you make a mistake at work.** You are now scared and negative thoughts hammered you- **"I'm so stupid". "I'm going to get fired."** Here the cognitive distortion is all-or-nothing thinking. As a person you make a mistake and either you are stupid or are not. Now it is your turn to challenge the negative thought. Ask yourself if there is any evidence to support the negative thought. Is it really true that you are stupid? Have you made mistakes in the past and still been successful? Is it possible that everyone makes mistakes? Now you replace the negative thought with a more realistic one such as **"I made a mistake at work, but that doesn't mean I'm stupid. Everyone makes mistakes. I can learn from this mistake and do better next time."** This can help you develop a more balanced and realistic perspective about yourself.

Distracting Attention:

Sometimes, the best way to deal with negative self-talk is to distract yourself from it. It is like avoiding the events or the place of occurrences that lead to negative thoughts. Engage yourself in activities that you enjoy much. You may go for a long drive with near and dear, and enjoy listening to music. Reading a book is one of the best remedies to get rid of negative self-talk. Engagement in physical exercises or going for a walk is found beneficial in such a situation. Never feel yourself alone in the journey to positive awareness. Feel that omnipresent God is with you, He wants you to win over negativity with full confidence.

However, never forget that managing negative self-talk takes practice and patience. Time is a great leveler. You will succeed in your mission and believe in yourself. Be kind to yourself and keep working on developing a more positive inner dialogue.

The Power of Positive Thinking:

"Positive thinking is more than just a tagline. It changes the way we see the world and ourselves. It allows us to approach life with optimism, confidence, and hope." - Harvey Mackay

(Harvey Mackay is an American businessman, and author of seven New York Times bestselling books, including three number-one bestsellers: *Swim with the Sharks Without Being Eaten Alive* (1988), *Beware the Naked Man Who Offers You His Shirt* (1992), and *Dig Your Own Well Before You Get Thirsty* (1997) **and** syndicated columnist.)

Positive thinking is the product of a positive mindset which can change the perception of our understanding of the circumstances. The Power of Positive Thinking is a concept that suggests that having a positive attitude and mindset can lead to greater success, happiness, and overall well-being. This idea is often associated with the work of **Norman Vincent Peale,** who wrote a book with the same title in 1952.

<u>The basic concept of positive thinking is that what you focus much you get that. The intensity of your positive emotions and thoughts can reverse your negative energy into positive</u>. When you focus on positive thoughts and attitudes, you can attract positive outcomes and experiences into your life. This can be achieved through techniques such as affirmations, visualization, and positive self-talk.

Research has shown that positive thinking can have numerous benefits, including improved mental health, increased resilience, and better coping skills in the face of challenges. It can also lead to better physical and mental health. Studies have found that positive emotions are associated with a lower risk of cardiovascular disease and other health problems. There is a growing body of scientific research that supports the power of positive thinking. Positive thinking can also help us to cope with stress more effectively and to achieve our goals. You might have read or heard the idiom "Birds of a feather flock together." What is its exact meaning? This means that people with similar interests, personalities, feelings, or backgrounds tend to associate with each other. Now it is clear that people with positive mindsets and thinking shall attract people of positive energy and positive thinking. Positivity is the symbol of progress and negativity is the symbol of backwardness and death. Nurturing positive thinking is the best solution to win over negative self-talk and negative thoughts. Let us take some examples of the power of positive thinking in action:

- *A student who believes in themselves and their ability to succeed is more likely to excel in school.*

- *An athlete who has a positive attitude is more likely to perform at their best.*

- *A person who is positive and hopeful is more likely to recover from a serious illness.*

Human history is the witness of people who have excelled in their lives through positive thinking and positive actions. However, it is important to note that positive thinking is a way but is not a cure-all and should not be used to ignore or avoid difficult emotions or situations. It is also not a substitute for seeking professional help when needed.

Chapter: 7

The Art of Saying No

Setting Boundaries and Saying No with Confidence:

"Saying no is an essential part of self-care. It's okay to say no to things that don't align with your values, priorities, or energy levels." - Rachel Hollis (She is an American motivational speaker, author, and businesswoman).

Saying no is an art or skill? Being social in the first instance, saying no is very difficult and one may feel guilty. Before proceeding further, you may have a question in mind what is the necessity to say no to others? It is natural to ask such a question. The answer is very simple, for the sake of self-care and well-being. If you love yourself in the true sense you have to learn the art of saying no. Successful people have learned this art from the very beginning. Mark Manson an American self-help author and blogger rightly says; **"Saying no is an important skill to learn, but it's not always easy. It's okay to feel uncomfortable at first, but the more you practice saying no, the easier it will become."** You have to practice it for a better future, and better relationships. For this purpose, you have to set boundaries and say no with confidence to maintain healthy relationships and prioritize your own needs and well-being.

The following tips can help you set boundaries and say no with confidence:

1. Identify your Boundaries:

Identify your boundaries involving your values and priorities that are important to you. Because you are the central point of discussions and attractions. Boundaries may include limits on your precious time, energy, or resources. Further, most importantly you should earmark your emotional boundaries, which you are willing to tolerate in your relationships. When you are drawing a *Laxman Rekha* of emotional boundaries, you have to be careful a little bit.

2. Communicate Clearly and Assertively:

Further, communicating your needs and priorities in clear terms is important. It must be assertive nature. Use "I" statements to express your feelings and needs, and be direct about your limits and boundaries. For example, financially you are sound but for the time being you are not in a comfortable position to lend. Someone near and dear came to you and asked for financial help to meet an urgent expenditure. Now you are definitely in a spot. In such a complicated situation, the only option left to you is to politely say "Sorry I am not in a position to help you." Your gesture may not hurt your friend, rather he will understand that you are right.

3. **Practice Self-care:**

Saying no and setting boundaries can be difficult, especially if you're used to putting others' needs before your own. You may not render selfless service on every occasion at the expense of your own interests and needs. In Indian homes, mothers take care of all the family members and neglect their well-being. It may be great for the family but harmful to the self-growth of the mothers. Practice self-care to help build your confidence and resilience, and make it easier to prioritize your own needs. Unless you understand your own needs you may not be able to set boundaries of priorities, resources, and needs.

4. **Positive Affirmations:**

Positive affirmations can help you build confidence and reinforce your boundaries. Some examples of positive affirmations are as follows;

- "I am worthy of saying no."
- "I am worthy of respect."
- "I am allowed to say no without guilt or explanation."
- "Saying no is a sign of strength and self-respect."
- "Saying no allows me to focus on my priorities and energy."
- "Saying no helps me to protect my boundaries and well-being."

Repeat affirmations as per your comfort as many times as you can, preferably at the time of retiring to bed and at the time of leaving bed in the early morning. Affirmations give you the courage and dimension to focus on your objectives.

5. **Be Consistent:**

Setting boundaries and saying no can be challenging, but it's important to be consistent to establish healthy habits and reinforce your boundaries. Stick to your boundaries and say no when you need to, even if it feels uncomfortable at first. Consistencies can be a habit that may lead to your goals and fulfillment.

Remember, setting boundaries and saying no with confidence is an important part of self-care and building healthy relationships. Prioritizing your own needs and communicating them clearly and assertively, are very important and can create the space and boundaries you need for your well-being.

Overcoming Guilt and Obligation:

Guilt is a useless emotion. It serves no purpose except to punish us for our mistakes. It doesn't help us learn from our mistakes or move on from them. It just keeps us stuck in the past." -
Brené Brown

Guilt is a form of emotion that hunts everyone and if it is not controlled timely. Gradually it kills you from within if you dwelt in it, without letting it go away. Feeling guilty for a while and preparing to learn a lesson from it is fine. Let it leave there without guilt and not make it proceed further as an issue. The obligation is, however, connected with your heart. If you fail to oblige genuinely to anybody, then it may give rise to guilt. Both guilt and obligation can be powerful emotions that make it difficult to set boundaries, prioritize your own needs, and make decisions that are best for you.

Let you follow some tips for overcoming guilt and obligation:

1. **Recognize the Source of Your Guilt:** Take some time to reflect on the source of your guilt and obligation. Being a social animal, it is fair to feel guilt as without emotion you are not a human being. But identifying the source is essential to uproot it for your progress and well-being. Recognize these feelings from where they are coming? Is it from within, or are they coming from external sources, such as family, friends, or societal expectations? Let us see some examples of guilt;

   - *Breaking a promise:* For example, you might feel guilty if you promise to help a friend with a project but then forget.
   - *Lying to someone*: Even if you lied for a good reason, you may still feel guilty about it.
   - *Making a mistake*: Everyone makes mistakes, but some people feel guiltier about them than others.
   - *Disappointing someone:* If you don't live up to someone's expectations, you may feel guilty about it.

2. **Challenge Your Assumptions:** An assumption is something that you take for granted to be true without

any evidence or proof. It is sometimes based on your preconceived views or can be based on your own personal experiences, beliefs, and values, or they can be based on what you have been told by others. **Often, guilt and obligation are based on assumptions or beliefs that may not be accurate. Challenge these assumptions by asking yourself questions like "Is this really my responsibility?" or "What would happen if I said no?"**

3. **Practice Self-compassion:** When you are under the influence of guilt and obligation, you are under tremendous pressure which may impact your physical and mental health. It is a crucial period for you. Be kind and compassionate with yourself, even if you're struggling to overcome guilt and obligation. Remember that it's okay to prioritize your own needs and set boundaries and that you don't have to be perfect always.

4. **Seek Support:** When we share our apprehension, fear, or any wrongdoing with near and dear, we feel relaxed. Because it releases our emotions, reduces stress, and draws sympathy. It gives us mental support to overcome the grit and obligation if any. Likely you may reach out to trusted friends or family members for support. In acute cases, you may consider talking to a therapist or counselor who can help you work through your feelings and develop healthy coping strategies.

5. **Take Action:** It is better to take small steps toward setting boundaries and prioritizing your own needs, even if it feels uncomfortable or scary at first. For example, you are a respectful person in the locality, and local club people invited you to grace the occasion on the annual day, but you are not comfortable attending

the function. Now you can take action as such; **"Thank you for the invitation, but I'm unable to attend."**

Remember, overcoming guilt and obligation is a process, and it may take time and effort to develop new habits and ways of thinking. But by challenging your assumptions, practicing self-compassion, and taking action to prioritize your own needs, you can create a healthier, more fulfilling life for yourself.

The Benefits of Prioritizing Your Time and Energy:

The most precious thing on the earth for humankind is time. Time is very punctual and can't wait for anybody for even a fraction of a second. You may not conserve it with any highly sophisticated devices, but you can intelligently spend it for the highest benefit for humanism and your well-being. For the highest gain from the time you have to learn to manage time. Prioritizing your time and energy can have numerous benefits for your physical, mental, and emotional well-being. Some of the key benefits include;

1. ***Increased Productivity:*** When you prioritize your tasks and activities which are most important can increase productivity. It may be on a daily or weekly basis. By focusing on the most important tasks you properly utilize time and energy, leading to a more productive environment, and avoid wasting time on less important or low-value activities.

2. ***Reduced Stress***: Proper time management leads to proper utilization of time and energy that completes the

tasks on time. By prioritizing your time and energy, you can reduce feelings of being overwhelmed and stressed by focusing on what's most important.

3. ***<u>Improved Work-Life balance:</u>*** In social life relationships and commitments are important for humans. By prioritizing your time and energy, you can create a better balance between your work, personal, and social life, and avoid burning out or neglecting important relationships or activities.

4. ***<u>Increased Self-awareness:</u>*** When you prioritize your time and energy you not only improve the output but also input in the shape of self-awareness. By taking the time to prioritize your time and energy, you can develop a greater sense of self-awareness and clarity around your goals, values, and priorities.

5. ***<u>Enhanced Creativity and Innovation</u>***: Time and energy management is also associated with creativity and innovation. When you enjoy quality time your mind engages in creative thinking which can give you an extra edge against your opponents. By prioritizing your time and energy, you can create more space and freedom to explore new ideas and opportunities.

6. ***<u>Improved Overall Well-being:</u>*** The human race is on the path to developing the overall well-being of every individual. The path to the goals may be different. But by prioritizing your time and energy, you can create a more fulfilling, satisfying life that aligns with your values and goals, and that supports your overall well-being and happiness.

Remember, prioritizing your time and energy is a skill that can be developed with practice and intention. Start by identifying your top priorities and focusing your time and energy on those tasks and activities that are most important and meaningful to you. Over time, you can build habits and systems that support your goals and help you create a healthier, successful, and more fulfilling life.

Chapter: 8

Embracing Your Own Path and Purpose

The Power of Ignoring the Opinions of Others:

The thing that most hurt many is the unwarranted and false allegations of others. Barring a few enlightened and intelligent people almost all people make opinions against others without knowing facts and without any gain. But, sometimes your opponents use such tricks to demoralize you to their advantage. When you are in setbacks many people may create many negative opinions about your character, performance, action-taking abilities, awareness, talent, etc. Even the people are not aware of your talent, creative awareness, honesty, and devotion to work make negative opinions that are very difficult to accept.

The power of ignoring the opinions of others is the ability to live your life on your own terms, free from the constraints of other people's expectations and judgments. It is the ability to pursue your dreams and goals, even if they are different from what others think you should be doing. When you ignore the opinions of others, you are not saying that you don't care about them or that their feedback is not valuable. Rather, you are saying that you are ultimately responsible for your own life and that you will make your own decisions based on your values and goals.

However, constructive criticism and opinion are always well come. The opinions of others can have a significant impact on our thoughts, feelings, and actions-taking process. While it's essential to listen to feedback and consider other people's viewpoints, it's equally important to know when to ignore their opinions.

Here are a few reasons why ignoring the opinions of others can be powerful:

- **It Allows You to Follow Your Intuition:** When you listen to the opinions of others too much, you may end up doubting your instincts. By ignoring other people's opinions, you can trust yourself more and make decisions based on what feels right for you.

- **It Helps You Stay True to Your Values:** When you focus too much on what other people think, you may compromise your own beliefs and values. Ignoring their opinions can help you stay true to what you believe in and make decisions that align with your values.

- **It can Increase Your Confidence:** When you rely too much on the opinions of others, you may feel unsure of yourself and lack confidence in your abilities. Ignoring their opinions can help you build confidence in yourself and trust your judgment. When you make your own decisions and live your life on your own terms, you begin to develop a stronger sense of self-confidence. You know that you are capable of making good choices and that you don't need the approval of others to feel good about yourself.

- **Reduced Stress and Anxiety**: Worrying about what other people think of you can be a major source of stress and anxiety. In this mortal world as an individual, you can't satisfy everyone. When you let go of the need to please everyone, you can finally relax and enjoy your life. I have faced such a situation in the past and suffered a lot.

- **Greater Creativity and Innovation:** When you are not afraid to be yourself and pursue your own ideas, you are more likely to be creative and innovative. You are not limited by the expectations of others, and you are free to explore new possibilities. When you try to find an unconventional path to pursue a goal it may attract different opinions from others.

- **More Fulfilling Relationships:** When you are not constantly trying to be someone you're not, you can build more authentic and fulfilling relationships with others. People will respect you for who you are, and you will be able to connect with them on a deeper level.

It is important to note that ignoring the opinions of others doesn't mean being dismissive or disrespectful. It's still essential to listen to feedback, consider other perspectives, and be open to learning from others. However, knowing when to trust your instincts, stay true to your values, and have confidence in yourself is equally important.

Strategies for Embracing Your Own Path and Purpose:

Embracing your own path and purpose can be a challenging but rewarding journey. It means living your life in a way that is true to yourself and your values and pursuing your dreams and goals, even if they are different from what others expect of you. It also means being accepting of yourself for who you are, flaws and all. You can live your own life not the expected lives of others. In many countries and cultures, sons and daughters are compelled to follow the wishes and desires of their parents against their own interests and self-conviction. Here you can find challenges are more complex.

There are many benefits to embracing your own path and purpose. When you are living a life that is aligned with your values and goals, you are more likely to be happy and fulfilled. You are also more likely to be successful in your career and relationships.

Here are some tips for embracing your own path and purpose:

1. **Get to Know Yourself**: What are your values? What are your strengths and weaknesses? What are your passions? The more you know about yourself, the better equipped you will be to make choices that are aligned with your true self. You can do this by reflecting on your past experiences, taking personality tests, and talking to people who know you well.

2. **Explore Your Interests:** What do you enjoy doing? What are you curious about? Try new things and see what you're good at. The more you explore, the more likely you are to find your passions.

3. **Set Goals:** What do you want to achieve in life? Once you know what you want, you can start to set goals and make a plan to achieve them. Your goals should be specific, measurable, achievable, relevant, and time-bound.

4. **Take Action**: Without taking action toward achieving goals is meaningless and it is just a dream. Don't just wait for things to happen. Take steps toward your goals, even if they are small steps. Remember every step counts. Drops of water create the ocean.

5. **Practice Self-care:** Taking care of your physical, mental, and emotional health is crucial to staying focused and motivated. Make sure you are getting enough sleep, eating a healthy diet on time, and finding ways to manage stress. Note it down without taking self-care, you can't achieve your goals. Never forget that self-care is associated with your personal goal because everything that you want to achieve is for the betterment of yourself first.

6. **Be Persistent:** There will be setbacks along the way. Don't give up on your dreams. Keep moving forward, even if it is slowly. Try to be on the track. Remember Albert Einstein the famous scientist once said-"Never give up on what you really want to do. The person with big dreams is more powerful than one with all the facts."

7. **Keep Learning and Growing:** Human life is a blessing of God for learning and transforming the same into action. Embracing your own path and purpose

involves continuous learning and growth. Make time to read valuable books, attend workshops, and engage in other activities that help you learn and grow.

8. **Surround Yourself with Supportive People:** Find people who believe in you and who support your goals. It will be difficult to achieve your goals without a strong support system. Having a supportive network of friends and family will make it easier to stay on track. Good people mean positive vibrations. When you are with people of positive thinking and energy you are more likely to get enough positive energy to perform better.

9. **Don't be Afraid to be Different**: It's important to remember that you are unique and special. Don't be afraid to follow your own path, even if it's different from what others are doing. Somebody says- ***"Don't be afraid to be different. Be afraid of being the same as everyone else."*** Be yourself as you are a unique creation of the universe. Never doubt your efficiencies and creative awareness in you.

Here are some examples of people who have embraced their own path and purpose:

- ***<u>Oprah Winfrey:</u>*** You know Oprah Winfrey is an American talk show host, actress, producer, and philanthropist. She is best known for her talk show, *The Oprah Winfrey Show*, which was the highest-rated television program of its kind in history and was nationally syndicated for 25 years from 1986 to 2011. However, she grew up in poverty and faced many challenges in her life. However, she never gave up on her dreams and she proved her.

- ***J.K. Rowling:*** J.K. Rowling is a British author and philanthropist best known for writing the Harry Potter fantasy series. The books have won multiple awards and sold more than 500 million copies, becoming the best-selling book series in history. Do you know her struggle in her early career? She was a single mother living on welfare when she wrote the first Harry Potter book. She was rejected by 12 different publishers before her book was finally accepted. However, she never gave up on her dream, and the Harry Potter series went on to become one of the most successful book series of all time.

- ***Steve Jobs:*** Steve Jobs was a college dropout who started Apple Computer in his garage. He was fired from Apple in the 1980s, but he returned to the company in the 1990s and led it to become one of the most successful technology companies in the world.

These are just a few examples of people who have embraced their own path and purpose. If you are struggling to find your own path, know that you are not alone. There are many resources available to help you on your journey. You should have a growth mindset to go forward in learning to achieve your dream goals.

Remember, embracing your own path and purpose is a journey, and it's okay to make mistakes and take detours along the way. What's important is that you stay true to yourself, never pretend you and keep moving forward.

Tips for Finding Your Passion and Staying True to Yourself:

Finding your passion and staying true to yourself can be a lifelong journey, but it's also a journey that can be incredibly rewarding. Find the things that excite you and that is the divine factor called passion. Your passion is your life that can transform you as well as others. Here are some tips to help you find your passion and stay true to yourself:

Explore Your Interests: Take some time to explore different activities and hobbies that fascinate you. Try new things and don't be afraid to step outside of your comfort zone.

Identify Your Strengths: Make a list of your strengths and the things you are good at. This can help you identify potential career paths or hobbies that align with your strengths.

Listen to Your Inner Voice: Pay attention to the things that make you feel alive and fulfilled. Listen to your inner voice and trust your intuition. Your inner voice is always true to yourself and that is aligned to your heart.

Don't be Afraid to Take Risks: Pursuing your passion often requires taking risks and stepping into the unknown. Don't be afraid to take a leap of faith and try something new. Remember risk-taking may cost you financial loss and wastage of valuable time. Take a calculated risk.

Surround Yourself with Positive Influences: Surround yourself with people who support and encourage you on your journey. Avoid negative influences that may discourage you or lead you off track. Encouragement sometimes makes wonders in an individual's life, however, the inner voice is supreme.

Stay True to Your Values: Your passion should align with your values and beliefs. Make sure you are staying true to yourself and not compromising your values to pursue your passion. For example, your values revolve around honesty, integrity, compassion, respect for others and responsibility are likely to be reflected in work, relationships, and behavior.

Keep Learning and Stay Focused on Your Goals: Pursuing your passion involves continuous learning. Keep your goals in mind and stay focused on the end result. Stay motivated by tracking your progress and celebrating your successes along the way.

Remember, finding your passion and staying true to yourself is a journey, and it may take some time to figure out what truly resonates with you. Keep an open mind, stay curious, focus on the objective, and trust the process.

Chapter: 9

Finding Space for Creativity and Connection

The Impact of Social Media and Technology on Creativity and Connection:

In the age of Social media and technology, we can't live even a few minutes without them. They have had both positive and negative impacts on creativity and connection. On the positive side, social media and technology have made it easier than ever to connect with people from all over the world and to share creative ideas and content. Platforms like Instagram, LinkedIn, Medium, TikTok, Facebook, and YouTube have given creators a platform to share their work and reach a global audience. Additionally, technology has provided artists and creatives with new tools and software that can enhance their work and help them bring their visions to life.

However, there are also negative impacts to consider. Social media can be a double-edged weapon when it comes to creativity, as it can both inspire and stifle creativity. On one hand, exposure to a wide range of content and ideas can be inspiring and lead to an arena of new creative vision. On the other hand, the pressure to constantly produce organic content can be challenging.

Additionally, social media and technology can have negative impacts on connection. While it's easier than ever to connect with others online, these connections are often shallow and lacking in depth. Social media can also contribute to feelings of loneliness and isolation, as people may feel like they are missing out on experiences that others are sharing online.

Furthermore, social media algorithms and the ability to curate our own online experience can contribute to echo chambers, where we only see content and ideas that align with our existing beliefs and values. This can limit our exposure to new ideas and perspectives and lead to a lack of diverse viewpoints.

In summary, social media and technology have had a significant impact on creativity and connection. While they offer many opportunities for inspiration and connection, at the same time potential negative impacts can't be ruled out. It is essential to use them mindfully and intelligently to promote creativity and connection in our lives.

Strategies for Ignoring Social Media and Technology:

Social media and technology can be powerful tools for creativity and connection. But it's important to be mindful of their potential negative impacts on our lives. Set the tone as and when necessary you can take breaks from them when needed. Decide intelligently, and let you conquer the negative impact of social media and technology not them conquer you.

Some strategies have been given below for ignoring social media and technology as and when necessary.

Set Boundaries: Set specific times of the day when you allow yourself to use social media and technology, and stick to those boundaries. This can help you save time, and stay more focused and mindful in your daily life.

Turn off Notifications: Turn off notifications for social media and other apps that tend to distract you. This can help you avoid the temptation to constantly check your phone and stay focused on other tasks.

Delete Apps: You can find some apps on your mobile that are disturbing and misleading. If you find such types of apps are causing you stress or anxiety, consider deleting them from your phone altogether.

Find Alternative Activities: Instead of scrolling through social media, find other activities that bring you joy and fulfillment. This could include reading a good book, going for a walk, or spending quality time with loved ones.

Practice Mindfulness: Mindfulness can help you stay present and centered, even with distractions. Consider practicing meditation or other mindfulness techniques to help you stay focused and centered throughout the day.

Set goals: Setting specific goals for yourself can help you stay motivated and focused on other tasks besides social media and technology.

Create a Positive Support System: Surround yourself with people who support your decision to take breaks from social media and technology. Having a support system can make it easier to stick to your boundaries and stay accountable. Remember creativity is your lifeline, it is running in your blood, not social media. In fact, unless you leave social media you can't be creative in the true sense. Your creativity starts when you leave social media.

Taking breaks from social media and technology is your compulsion, not luxury. But it doesn't mean you have to completely give them up. It's all about finding a balance that works for you and helps you stay focused on what truly matters in your life.

The Benefits of Disconnecting and Finding Space for Creativity:

In the fast-changing world disconnecting and finding space for creativity can have numerous benefits, and be rewarding. They may include;

Improved Mental Health: Disconnecting from technology can help you to reduce stress, anxiety, and depression. Studies have shown that spending too much time on screens can lead to increased feelings of loneliness, isolation, and dissatisfaction with life. Taking breaks from technology can help to improve your mood, boost your energy levels, and make you feel more connected to the world around you.

Enhanced Creativity: When you're not constantly bombarded with stimuli from screens, your mind has more space to wander and come up with new ideas. Creativity is often sparked by boredom, so giving yourself some time to disconnect can help boost your creative awareness.

Improved Focus and Productivity: By disconnecting, you allow yourself to focus on one task at a time without being distracted by notifications or other interruptions. This can improve your productivity and help you accomplish more in less time.

Better Sleep: Research has shown that exposure to the blue light emitted by electronic devices can disrupt sleep patterns. By disconnecting before bedtime, you can improve the quality of your sleep and wake up feeling more refreshed.

Enhanced Relationships: It has been proved on so many occasions that social media has more or less taken personal relationships to a reasonably low level. Disconnecting can allow you to spend more quality time with loved ones and strengthen your relationships.

Greater Appreciation for the Simple Things in Life: When you're not constantly checking your phone or computer, you're more likely to notice and appreciate the little things in life, such as a beautiful sunset, a beautiful butterfly in the garden, a delicious meal, reading a poem or short story from a weekly magazine, or a meaningful conversation with a friend.

Be practical in life. Think about your creative awareness and God-given talent. You may not spoil your talent running behind the mirage impact of social media. Take some time to introspect and take a break from social media and technology to find space for creativity. It can have numerous benefits for both your mental and physical well-being. Your small but meaningful actions can help you recharge, increase your creativity, improve your productivity, and enhance your relationships with others.

Chapter: 10

Navigating Current Events without Getting Overwhelmed

The Impact of the News Cycle on Mental Health:

The news cycle can have a significant impact on mental health. Exposure to constant negative news can lead to stress, anxiety, depression, and many complicated situations.

Increased Anxiety and Stress: One reason why the news cycle especially those related to violence, terrorism, war, natural disasters, and pandemics can be so harmful to mental health is that it can activate the **_"fight or flight"_** response. This is a natural physiological response to danger, but when it is triggered too often, it can lead to chronic stress. Chronic stress can have a number of negative consequences for mental and physical health, including distractions in the sleep cycle, anxiety, depression, and insomnia.

Heightened Fear and Trauma: Repeated exposure to traumatic events through news coverage can lead to increased fear and trauma, especially for individuals who have experienced similar events in the past. This can lead to a variety of mental health issues, such as post-traumatic stress disorder (PTSD). We have all experienced such types of horrific experiences during the pandemic Covid 19.

Overwhelming Feelings of Helplessness and Hopelessness: The sheer volume of news stories and the continuous cycle of negativity can leave individuals feeling overwhelmed and helpless, leading to feelings of hopelessness and a sense that there is nothing that can be done to improve the situation. Such helplessness creates a feeling of insecurity in the mind leading to self-sabotaging.

Increased Polarization and Division: News coverage can contribute to increased polarization and division among different groups, leading to a sense of hostility and mistrust toward others. Even during a war-like situation, news reporting becomes challenging and biased. The media houses of different states supporting news agencies give controversial and contrasting news leading to confusion in the minds of viewers.

Decreased Resilience: Constant exposure to negative news can decrease resilience and coping skills, making it more difficult for individuals to manage stress and anxiety.

It is important to be mindful of the impact that the news cycle can have on mental health and to take steps to manage exposure to negative news when necessary without being overwhelmed.

Strategies for Staying Informed Without Getting Overwhelmed:

In today's world, it's easy to become overwhelmed by the sheer volume of information available to us at our fingertips. With social media, news outlets, and blogs all vying for our attention, it can be challenging to stay informed without feeling like we're drowning in a sea of information. Here are some strategies to help you stay informed without getting overwhelmed:

Take breaks: It's okay to take a break from the news and social media. Give yourself permission to unplug and focus on other things, like spending time with family and friends, pursuing hobbies, wandering in nature, or doing some physical exercise. If you have a garden you may engage sometime to get fresh and energetic.

Limit your news intake: It is important to stay informed about the world around you, but you don't need to consume every single news story. Set a time limit for how much time you spend consuming news each day. Try not to exceed 30-60 minutes, and avoid checking your phone for updates every few minutes.

Multiple Authentic Sources: Stick to trusted news sources that have a reputation for accuracy and unbiased reporting. Avoid sensationalized or clickbait headlines that are designed to get clicks rather than giving you the right information. Get news from two to three authentic sources to get a well-rounded view of a story. This can help you avoid biases and better understand different perspectives.

Be selective with social media: Be mindful of the social media accounts you follow and how much time you spend on them. Avoid getting sucked into a cycle of doom-scrolling or getting caught up in debates or arguments. Remember social media is like a double-edged weapon. Be careful of its use.

Prioritize what's important: Focus on the news that's most relevant to you and your life. It is not necessary that you have to read every article or watch every news segment. Be mindful of how the news makes you feel. If you start to feel anxious, stressed, or overwhelmed, take a break from the news. Go for a walk, listen to music, or do something else that you enjoy. Talk to someone you trust about how you are feeling. Talking about your feelings can help you to process them and cope with stress.

Seek professional help: If you are struggling to cope with the impact of the news cycle on your mental health you may seek professional help. A therapist can help you to develop healthy coping mechanisms and manage your symptoms.

It is important to remember that you are not alone. Many people are struggling with the impact of the news cycle on their mental health. There are resources available to help you cope. If you are struggling, please reach out for help.

Remember, it's not about staying informed at all costs. It's about finding a balance between staying informed and taking care of your mental health. Take care of your primary task first and getting updated news is secondary. By implementing these strategies, you can stay informed without getting overwhelmed.

Tips for Maintaining Perspective and Finding Balance:

Perspective in life is the way you view the world and your place in it. It is your unique outlook on life, shaped by your experiences, beliefs, and values. Your perspective influences how you interpret events involving you, make informed decisions, your behavior, and interact with others.

A positive perspective can help you to see the good in people and situations, even when things are difficult and not going as you expect. It can also help you to stay motivated and resilient in the face of challenges. A negative perspective, on the other hand, can lead to pessimism, cynicism, and self-criticism. It can also make it more difficult to cope with stress and setbacks.

It is important to note that your perspective is not fixed. You are the sole owner of yourself and can choose to shift your perspective at any time. This can be helpful if you find yourself feeling stuck in a negative mindset.

Maintaining perspective and finding balance in your life are essential for overall well-being. When we have perspective, we can see the bigger picture and understand that our problems are often not as big as they seem. When we are balanced, we can give our time and energy to the people and things that are most important to us.

Here are some tips to help you maintain perspective and find balance:

Focus on what's important: Sometimes we run after unnecessary things ignoring our true value. Identify your values, and priorities and focus on what's important. Once you know your values, and priorities you can start to make decisions and set goals that align with them. Make sure you're spending your time and energy on the things that matter most to you.

Practice gratitude: Take time each day to reflect on the things you're grateful for. Gratitude can help you maintain perspective and keep things in balance. Amy Collette says-**"Gratitude is a powerful catalyst for happiness. It's the spark that lights a fire of joy in your soul**." Be grateful for what you have the doors for a bright future will be opened. *Remember what you have millions are asking for that and never feel deprived and be thankful for the things you have*.

Take care of your physical health: Practice self-love. Exercise regularly, eat a healthy diet, and get enough sleep. When your body is healthy, your mind is calm and quiet. A calm and cool mind can maintain balance and perspective easily.

Set boundaries: It is important to set boundaries between your professional life, personal life, and social life. This will help you to avoid overcommitting yourself and to have time for the things that are most important to you. It is okay to say no to requests from others, especially if you are already feeling overwhelmed.

Practice mindfulness: Practice mindfulness techniques like meditation, deep breathing, etc. These techniques can help you stay present and maintain a positive perspective.

Connect with others: Spend time with family and friends who support you and help you maintain perspective. Cultivate positive relationships that lift you up and help you stay balanced.

Take time for self-care: Take time each day to do something that you enjoy, like reading, listening to music, or taking a relaxing bath. Nature is the treasure house of beauty and wellness. You can explore that to your advantage. Self-care can help you recharge and maintain balance.

Remember, finding balance and maintaining perspective is an ongoing process. Be patient with yourself, and don't be afraid to adjust your approach as needed. By implementing these tips, you can find balance and maintain perspective in your life.

Chapter: 11

The Art of Ignoring for Inner Peace and Contentment

The Power of Ignoring for Inner Peace and Contentment:

"Ignoring negative people and situations is a powerful tool for protecting your energy and well-being." – Unknown

The power of ignoring for inner peace and contentment is a powerful tool that can help you reduce stress, anxiety, and negativity in your life. What I feel negative thoughts, emotions, and negative elements in our lives make us misled into melancholy. The ultimate objectives of every life are joy and happiness. When you learn to ignore certain things, you are essentially choosing to focus your energy on the things that are important to you and that bring you joy. This can lead to a more productive, peaceful, and fulfilling life.

Here are some ways that ignoring can be beneficial:

1. **Ignore negativity:** Ignoring negative people is not your fault, rather it is a blessing in disguise. When you encounter negative people or situations, sometimes the best thing you can do is ignore them. Don't make any argument with them. The negative vibration of the negative people may irritate you, and hurt you much but now you are trained enough to ignore them and leave the place if warranted. They may criticise you at your behind but don't let negativity consume your thoughts and emotions. Instead, ignore them as if nothing has happened and focus on positive things and people in your life.

2. **Ignore distractions:** In today's digital age, it's easy to become distracted by social media, emails, and other notifications. But of the digital distractions, you may find other external distractions like the noise of vehicular movement, crowds, factories, etc. Ignoring these distractions can help you focus on the task at hand and be more productive.

3. **Ignore criticism:** Everybody is prone to criticism. Even the prophets, seers, and Gods have been subjected to criticism by the unscrupulous elements of the society. Create neutral views on criticism even if not all criticism is constructive. Sometimes, people may criticize you out of jealousy or insecurity. Learn to ignore this type of criticism and focus on constructive feedback that can help you grow.

4. **Ignore the past:** It is a great tip for you to ignore the unhappy past. Learn lessons from the same but dwelling on past mistakes and regrets can prevent you from moving forward and achieving inner peace. Learn to let go of the past and focus on the present moment.

Nobody sees the future and the only present is to cherish. The present moment is only yours, never spoil this running after the past and mirage of the future.

5. **Ignore comparison:** Comparing yourself to others can lead to feelings of inadequacy and discontent. Remember you are unique and have the potential to achieve the success you dream of. Learn to appreciate your own unique qualities and talents and focus on your own journey.

It's important to note that ignoring doesn't mean avoiding or denying problems that need to be addressed. It simply means choosing to focus on the positive and not allowing negative thoughts and emotions to consume you. By practicing the power of ignoring, you can achieve inner peace and contentment in your life.

Techniques for Cultivating a Mindset of Ignoring:

"The only way to escape the noise of others is to silence the noise within yourself."

– Deepak Chopra

Cultivating a mindset of ignoring can be challenging, especially if you're used to giving attention to everything that crosses your path. The external noise that surrounds us can be overwhelming. However, the most disruptive noise is often the chatter in our own minds.

We can learn to silence this internal noise by practicing mindfulness, meditation, etc.

Here are some techniques that can help you cultivate a mindset of ignoring:

Practice mindfulness: Mindfulness involves being present and aware of your thoughts and surroundings. It can help you recognize when you're getting caught up in negative thoughts or distractions, so you can choose to ignore them and focus on the present moment. When you are mindful, you are less likely to get caught up in negative thoughts or ruminations. There are many different ways to practice mindfulness, such as meditation, yoga, or simply taking a few minutes each day to focus on your breath.

Create a to-do list: Write down the things you need to do each day, with time slats so that you can stay focused on your priorities and ignore distractions that may come your way. Practice it religiously to get better results.

Develop a positive mindset: Cultivate a positive mindset by focusing on the good things in your life and practicing gratitude. If you count your success even the small, that can fuel positive energy in you. This can help you ignore negative thoughts and emotions that can hold you back.

Set boundaries: Set boundaries. It is important to set boundaries with people and things that drain your energy or make you feel bad about yourself. This may mean saying no to requests, limiting your exposure to certain people or situations, or taking breaks from social media. This can help you ignore distractions and negativity that don't serve you.

Practice self-care: Take care of yourself by getting enough sleep, eating a healthy diet, and exercising regularly. When you feel good, it's easier to cultivate a mindset of ignoring.

Identify your triggers. What are the things that typically cause you to feel stressed, anxious, or upset? Unless the doctor diagnoses a patient, the proper medication isn't possible. Identifying your trigger is like a diagnosis. Once you are aware of your triggers, you can start to develop strategies for avoiding or ignoring them.

Challenge negative thoughts: It is natural to have negative thoughts in your mind. When you have a negative thought, ask about its validity. Is there any evidence to support it? If not, challenge the thought and replace it with a more positive one.

Forgive yourself and others. Holding on to grudges and resentment can take a toll on your mental health. It is important to learn to forgive yourself and others for mistakes. This will help you to let go of negative emotions and move on.

It is important to note that ignoring does not mean pretending that something does not exist. It simply means choosing not to give it your attention and energy. When you learn to ignore the things that are not important to you, you can focus your energy on the things that are truly important to you. This can lead to a more peaceful and fulfilling life. Remember, cultivating a mindset of ignoring takes practice and patience. Don't expect to be perfect, but keep working on it.

The Benefits of Letting Go and Finding Contentment in the Present Moment:

Letting go and finding contentment in the present moment can have a variety of benefits for your mental and emotional well-being. Some of the key benefits include;

1. **Reduced stress and anxiety:** When you let go of worries and concerns about the past or future, you can reduce feelings of stress and anxiety. Focusing on the present moment can help you feel more calm and centered. No stress and anxiety means life is easy and filled with joy and happiness.

2. **Improved relationships**: Letting go of grudges, resentments, and negative emotions can improve your relationships with others. When you're not holding onto negative feelings, you can communicate more effectively and connect with others on a deeper level.

3. **Greater self-awareness:** By focusing on the present moment, you can become more aware of your thoughts, emotions, and physical sensations. This can help you better understand yourself and make positive changes in your life.

4. **Increased happiness and contentment:** When you find contentment in the present moment, you can experience greater happiness and satisfaction in life. You'll be less focused on what you don't have or what you're worried about, and more focused on what you do have and what's going well in your life.

5. **Improved mental and emotional health:** Letting go of negative thoughts and emotions can improve your mental and emotional health. You'll be less likely to experience symptoms of depression, anxiety, or other mental health conditions.

Overall, learning to let go and find contentment in the present moment can have numerous benefits for your well-being. It takes practice and patience, but with time, you can cultivate a more peaceful and fulfilling life.

Key Takeaways from the Book

CHAPTER: 1

1. Attentional control is the cognitive ability to regulate one's attention, focusing on specific tasks while ignoring distractions. It's crucial for various cognitive processes, daily activities, and social interactions. Brain regions like the prefrontal cortex, anterior cingulate cortex, and parietal cortex are associated with attentional control.

2. Spatial attention allows us to focus on specific locations in space, while orienting is the process of shifting attention to new locations. Endogenous orienting is goal-driven, while exogenous orienting is triggered by external stimuli. Spatial attention and orientation are vital for activities like driving, reading, and sports.

3. Attentional disorders like ADHD can impact a person's ability to regulate attention, impulses, and activity levels. ADHD is a neurodevelopmental condition with structural and neurotransmitter differences in the brain. Treatment may include medication, therapy, and lifestyle changes.

4. Selective attention is the ability to focus on relevant stimuli while ignoring irrelevant ones, crucial for tasks like driving, reading, and listening in noisy environments. Factors like motivation and emotion influence selective attention, and deficits can occur in conditions like ADHD and schizophrenia.

5. Working memory allows temporary storage and manipulation of information during tasks and is vital for complex cognitive functions. Training, lifestyle choices, and strategies like mnemonic devices can improve working memory.

6. Cognitive load refers to the mental effort required for tasks. Intrinsic, extraneous, and germane cognitive load types impact learning and cognitive performance. Managing cognitive load through task simplification and clear instructions is crucial for effective teaching and learning.

CHAPTER: 2

1. Ignoring distractions is crucial for improving focus, productivity, and overall well-being. Distractions, whether external or internal, can lead to stress, reduced decision-making quality, and hindered creativity.

2. By managing distractions through strategies like time management, a conducive work environment, setting boundaries with digital devices, practicing mindfulness, and using techniques like the Pomodoro Technique, you can significantly enhance your ability to stay focused on essential tasks.

3. The benefits include increased focus, reduced stress, better decision-making, heightened creativity, and improved relationships with others. Ignoring distractions allows you to accomplish your goals and lead a more fulfilling life.

CHAPTER: 3

1. Information overload is a modern challenge caused by an excess of available data, leading to stress, poor decision-making, reduced productivity, and burnout. Managing information overload involves learning to filter out irrelevant content, setting priorities, establishing boundaries, practicing mindfulness, and organizing information efficiently.

2. By developing strategies to prioritize information, individuals can make more informed decisions, maintain focus on critical tasks, and prevent feeling overwhelmed by the sheer volume of data in the information-rich world.

3. Effective prioritization and managing distractions are key to combating information overload and maintaining mental well-being.

CHAPTER: 4

1. Mindfulness is the practice of being fully present in the moment, helping individuals to focus, reduce distractions, improve concentration, and enhance creativity. It trains the mind to be present, reduces distractions, and enhances concentration.

2. Techniques for practicing mindfulness include mindful breathing, body scan meditation, mindful walking, mindful eating, and mindful visualization.

3. Acknowledging and labeling distractions can help individuals manage and ignore distractions more effectively. By making mindfulness a regular part of their daily routine and being patient with themselves, individuals can develop the art of ignoring distractions and improve their focus and overall well-being.

CHAPTER: 5

1. The key takeaway from this chapter is that finding a balance between attention and obligation is crucial for overall well-being and success.

2. Prioritizing your time, setting boundaries, and learning to say no are essential skills. It's important to focus on quality over quantity in your obligations and to be flexible when necessary.

3. Self-care and self-love are fundamental to fulfilling your obligations effectively, as a well-cared-for individual can give more and perform better. Managing your time efficiently, delegating tasks, and maintaining a realistic schedule can help you achieve your goals while maintaining balance in your life.

CHAPTER: 6

1. The impact of negative thoughts and self-talk on our mental and physical health, as well as our overall well-being, is profound. They can lead to

decreased self-esteem, increased anxiety and depression, poor coping skills, relationship problems, and physical health issues.

2. To combat negative self-talk, one can employ techniques such as mindfulness, positive affirmations, reframing thought patterns, cognitive restructuring, and distracting attention. These strategies can help shift from negative to positive thinking, which has been shown to improve mental health, resilience, coping skills, and overall well-being.

3. Positive thinking can lead to better outcomes and is a valuable tool in facing life's challenges.

CHAPTER: 7

1. Prioritizing your time and energy is a crucial skill for enhancing productivity, reducing stress, and achieving a better work-life balance. It allows you to become more self-aware, fostering creativity and innovation, ultimately leading to improved overall well-being.

2. By focusing on what truly matters and aligning your actions with your values and goals, you can lead a more fulfilling and satisfying life. Developing this skill requires practice and intention, as it empowers you to make the most of your limited time and energy resources, promoting a healthier and more successful life.

CHAPTER: 8

1. Embracing your own path and purpose involves self-discovery, setting clear goals, taking action, and persevering through setbacks. It's about knowing yourself, pursuing your passions, and staying true to your values. It requires surrounding yourself with positive influences and being unafraid to be different.

2. Embracing your own path may not be easy, but it's a rewarding journey that leads to personal fulfillment, authenticity, and a life aligned with your true self.

CHAPTER: 9

1. Disconnecting from social media and technology offers numerous benefits, including improved mental health, enhanced creativity, better focus and productivity, improved sleep, stronger relationships, and a greater appreciation for life's simple joys.

2. Finding space for creativity can help recharge your mind and lead to a more balanced and fulfilling life. It's essential to strike a balance between the digital world and the real world to harness these advantages and maintain a healthy and creative lifestyle.

CHAPTER: 10

1. The constant exposure to negative news, such as violence, disasters, and pandemics, can significantly impact mental health by increasing anxiety, stress, and feelings of helplessness. To mitigate these effects, it's essential to employ strategies for staying informed without becoming overwhelmed, such as setting time limits, choosing reliable news sources, and taking breaks from news consumption.

2. Additionally, maintaining perspective and finding balance in life is crucial for overall well-being. Focus on priorities, practice gratitude, take care of physical health, set boundaries, practice mindfulness, connect with supportive relationships, and prioritize self-care to maintain a positive perspective and balanced life.

CHAPTER: 11

1. Ignoring negativity, distractions, criticism, the past, and comparisons can lead to inner peace and contentment.

2. Cultivating a mindset of ignoring involves practicing mindfulness, setting boundaries, developing a positive mindset, practicing self-care, and challenging negative thoughts.

3. Letting go and finding contentment in the present moment can reduce stress, improve

relationships, enhance self-awareness, increase happiness, and improve mental and emotional health. Cultivating these practices can lead to a more peaceful and fulfilling life.

May I ask you for a small favor?

At the outset, I want to give a big thanks for taking out time to read this book. You could have chosen any other book, but you chose mine, and I totally appreciate this.

I hope you got at least a few actionable insights that will have a positive impact on your day-to-day life.

Can I ask for 30 seconds more of your time?

I would love it if you could leave a review about the book. Reviews may not matter to big-name authors; but they're a tremendous help for authors like me, who don't have many followers. They help me grow my readership by encouraging folks to take a chance on my books.

To put it straight, reviews are the lifeblood of any author.

"THE ART OF SELECTIVE ATTENTION,"

Please leave your review by visiting the **"Review Section** "of this book's page on Amazon.

It will just take less than a minute of your time, but will tremendously help me to reach out to more people, so please leave your review.

Thanks for your support of my work. And I would love to see your review.

DISCLAIMER

This book is for educational purposes only. Readers acknowledge that the author does not render legal, financial, medical, or professional advice. The content within this book has been derived from various sources. Please consult a licensed professional before attempting any techniques outlined in this book.

By reading this document, the reader agrees that under no circumstances is the author responsible for any direct or indirect losses incurred as a result of the use of the information contained within this document, including but not limited to errors, omissions, or inaccuracies.

Adherence to all applicable laws and regulations, including international, federal, state, and local governing professional licensing, business practices, advertising, and all other jurisdictions, is the sole responsibility of the purchaser or reader.

Neither the author nor the publisher assumes any responsibility or liability whatsoever on behalf of the purchaser or reader of these materials. Any perceived slight of any individual or organization is purely unintentional.